Born to Privilege

Rebecca Bryan-Howell

Copyright ©2020 by Rebecca Bryan-Howell
All rights reserved. No part of this book may be reproduced or transmitted in any form or by any means without written permission from the author.

Paperback ISBN: 978-1-7325959-2-7
eBook ISBN: 978-1-7325959-3-4
Library of Congress Control Number: 2020909587

Scripture quotations marked (KJV) are taken from The Holy Bible, King James Version. Public Domain.

Scripture quotations marked (NLT) are taken from The Holy Bible, New Living Translation, copyright ©1996, 2004, 2015 by Tyndale House Foundation. Used by permission of Tyndale House Publishers, a Division of Tyndale House Ministries, Carol Stream, Illinois 60188. All rights reserved.

Scripture quotations marked (NIV) are taken from The Holy Bible, New International Version®, NIV®. Copyright ©1973, 1978, 1984, 2011 by Biblica, Inc.™ Used by permission of Zondervan. All rights reserved worldwide, *www.zondervan.com*. The "NIV" and "New International Version" are trademarks registered in the United States Patent and Trademark Office by Biblica, Inc.™

Scripture quotations marked (BSB) are taken from The Holy Bible, Berean Study Bible. Copyright ©2016, 2018 by Bible Hub. Used by Permission. All Rights Reserved Worldwide.

Scripture quotations marked (GNT) are from the Good News Translation in Today's English Version- Second Edition. Copyright © 1992 by American Bible Society. Used by Permission.

Scripture quotations marked (ESV) are from The ESV® Bible (The Holy Bible, English Standard Version®), copyright ©2001 by Crossway, a publishing ministry of Good News Publishers. Used by permission. All rights reserved.

Published in the United States of America
By Rebecca Bryan-Howell
www.prismoflife.com

Dedication

This book is dedicated, first, to the original class of ladies whose commitment and loyalty supported my passion to share this vital message for women. Your eagerness drew from the depths of my soul every element to complete this study; your participation inspired me to create fun and relevant material; and your whole-hearted comradery kept the atmosphere of our gatherings vibrant and real from start to finish. To Rose, Kathy, Beverly, Terri, Carol, Lana, Suzie, and Sherie, I thank you for your friendship and consistency in pursuing God's Word together!

To all my family and friends who challenged me onward with their words of encouragement and enthusiasm, and all who wanted to attend the class but had other commitments: Your hopeful anticipation that I would do another class inspired me to write this book and share it with women everywhere.

To my faithful and amazing husband, Jim, who allowed me to glean from his own life experience for some of my illustrations; and who tirelessly supported me through this process—you are my hero! Your constant encouragement in helping me designate time for writing is another example of how willingly you support my dreams and love me for who God made me to be. Your wisdom and flexibility help me to balance my busy life; and I love you for it. Thank you from the bottom of my heart!

Most importantly going forward, I dedicate this Women's Bible Study to my readers for settling the score, once and for all, about who you really are and why you are actually here! My brimming hope and earnest prayer is that you will not only squeeze every last drop of nourishment from this study for your own health and beauty, but that when you finish the last chapter you will start over again in your own "Circle of Wagons" and share the wealth! Read the Preface to get your wheels rolling in the right direction, and dive right in! Because *YOU*, my dears, have been

Born to Privilege!

With all my Love,
Becca
imbeccafaith@gmail.com   www.prismoflife.com

Table of Contents

Preface	1
1. Beauty for Ashes	7
2. Chosen by God	19
3. Called Out: A Patent for Purpose	29
4. Charm School	41
5. Loyalty: The Vine and the Branches	59
6. Dressed for Battle	81
7. If the Crown Fits	109
8. Royal Counsel – New Normal	133
About the Author	158

Preface

Our world is brimming with varied and countless personality types and character combinations. Some people are unquestionably more self-motivated than others, but we can all use a little ETC – Encouragement to Continue – on our paths of Life because people need "people"! Interaction and relationship with others enhances our experience and provides a more balanced perspective. There is a priceless element of support for the journey when we encounter someone else who has had an experience similar to our own. C.S. Lewis said in his book, <u>The Four Loves</u>, "Friendship is born at that moment when one person says to another, 'What! You too? I thought I was the only one.'"[1]

I wrote about this occasion in a story called "Circle the Wagons" and, since friendship is a significant element of encouragement, I include it here as a warm and colorful opening to this book.

> There was one last cup of good coffee. I poured my mug full and thought about the day. It had been breezy; the weather was turning and summer days would soon be far behind. I did not want the winter to be harsh but I had a deep down hunch, wondering if it would be; and, if so, well…we had weathered harsh winters before. The day's conversation had brought back some of those memories, as well as renewed consolation that "there's nothing new under the sun," and after every winter comes the spring again.

---

[1] C.S. Lewis, "The Four Loves," First American Edition, (New York: Harcourt Brace and Co, 1960)

We kind of crammed these plans in our pockets at the last minute. Everybody was busy and we didn't know until nearly the day of whether it would work out to get together or not, but it did; and I felt happy as I watched my friends around my table enjoying my simple salad and sandwich lunch. I had to smile, seeing and hearing us interact again. These friends I have, they're just like a good book; the kind you can hardly put down and would be willing to miss sleep just to read another chapter. Then, when you finally have a chance to pick it up again, you jump right back into the momentum of the story. Our friendship is like that. The events of our lives weave together to make up some of the most intriguing pages you could ever read; and every session ends with, "...to be continued." Whenever we get together we always tell our kids and hubbies that we'll be home in a little while; but the more we "read", the harder it is to "put down the book". Our search for "a good stopping place" just gets us deeper into the plot.

We laugh together, we cry together, we talk with our hands and finish each other's sentences; and all the while something wonderful is happening. We're being filled up with a deep, inner richness that smooths out Life's rough edges and fills in the cracks of the dry, parched soul. We find gold mines together and we share the wealth. When the chapter is funny, the laughter that fills the room is a clear, bubbling brook that refreshes everyone. When the story is sober, and the cry of a wounded heart is heard, the tears of compassion flow all around; and in the tender, caring atmosphere of friendship, healing can begin. It's a connection that leaves no one on the outside. There is common ground where the feelings run strong and free; and the miracle of the truly kindred spirit touches everyone in the room, braiding us together like strands of a strong rope.

As I tipped my cup for the last sip, another picture filled my thoughts: wagons – prairie wagons circling the camp as the sun set and the darkness of night began to settle on the plains. We hear a lot about the pioneers of the Old West and how brave they were; about the many hardships they had to endure and the unimaginable sorrows they experienced. Yet I am convinced that the ones who made it all the way with hope to spare *knew the priceless value of friendship and sharing.* One wagon could easily fall prey to all the perils of the journey; but when a *company* of wagons encircled the camp there was not only comfort, security and strength – there was a big fire. It was the kind of blaze that sends warmth, light, and new hope in all directions; burning late into the night to keep the desert chill at bay and the creatures of the darkness back against the distant shadow of the hills.

There's not a human being anywhere who has never felt loneliness. Yet, there is a way to travel through life that takes the bite out of that word; and that is the way of friendship. The reason is because in the Circle of Wagons there is more of everything: more strength, more safety, more grub and more common sense. It can be a challenge to pull the circle together at times, but it's always worth the extra effort. There will be someone who has already been where you are going and who has already tasted what it's your turn to try. Someone who can fix what you've broken and patch what you've torn. Friends can see for you when the sun is in your eyes and pull you up when you're too weak to climb. They can give you hope when your barrel is empty and make you laugh when you want to cry.

And, if there *is* an attack, you are not alone to fight the battle.

> *We're pioneers, too!* I thought. *We've got a vision to fulfill and we have our prairie wagons loaded with hopes and dreams. We have the Trails of Life to travel with the storms, the varmints, and the unexpected turns…and we have the two most important ingredients of a successful journey: God to guide us, and friends to walk beside us.* As I glanced back at the clock and realized how quickly the time had passed I had one last comforting thought: *It's time for us to part, and face the next leg of the journey; but whether it's a field of flowers or a raging river it'll make a good story around the Fire of Friendship when the wagons circle once again.*

Having a circle of people to go through Life with is vital for ultimate success; not because other women have had that opportunity and laud it, nor because a brilliant psychologist or life coach has done the research and swears by it. It is important because it is God's idea! That is why our key verse for this Women's Bible Study comes from the tenth chapter of the book of Hebrews, verses 24 and 25: *"And let us consider how we may **spur one another on toward love and good deeds**, not giving up **meeting together**, as some are in the habit of doing, but **encouraging one another** – and all the more as you see the Day approaching"* (NIV).

I quote C.S. Lewis once again from his book, <u>The Four Loves</u>:

> In friendship...we think we have chosen our peers. In reality a few years' difference in the dates of our births, a few more miles between certain houses, the choice of one university instead of another...the accident of a topic being raised or not raised at a first meeting – any of these chances might have kept us

apart. But, for a Christian, there are, strictly speaking, no chances. A secret master of ceremonies has been at work. Christ, who said to the disciples, 'Ye have not chosen me, but I have chosen you,' can truly say to every group of Christian friends, 'Ye have not chosen one another but I have chosen you for one another.' The friendship is not a reward for our discriminating and good taste in finding one another out. It is the instrument by which God reveals to each of us the beauties of others.[2]

...to which I would venture to add "and the richness of a full life"! As children of God, we are re-born into lives of blessing and privilege because we have come into relationship with the creator of Life itself. Through this relationship with God, and only through this supernatural bond, do we gain access to all the wisdom and instruction he has provided for us to live life to the fullest; hence, the title of this book, *Born to Privilege*. In these pages, we will talk about what this means, and how understanding these principles will not only enable us to live strongly, happily and victoriously as individual women, but will automatically facilitate a Circle of Wagons for each of us. These circles, many of which will undoubtedly overlap, will provide the atmosphere of deep friendship within which we will not only find the necessary elements to grow and thrive on our pathways, but will also discover creative and rewarding ways to help and encourage others in the same exceptional initiative of learning and *choosing* to become the very best that we can be in this life.

---

[2] C.S. Lewis, "The Four Loves"

Chapter 1: Beauty for Ashes

Some of the most famous stories of all time carry a "rags to riches" plot that pulls at the heartstrings of the reader and balances tears with smiles in a most satisfying way. As little girls, how many of us longed to be Cinderella? But with maturity and a bit of life experience we came to realize that even though the "riches" part sounded like the perfect dream-come-true, the "rags" part was the undesirable qualifier that fed the passion behind the story. Sadness and rejection are the first reality before the heroine gets to wear a tiara or shiny slippers—any volunteers? If becoming a princess requires being a scullery maid dressed in ugly rags who suffers physical and verbal abuse every day, do we still want to go there? On the other hand, isn't that where the "happy endings" come from? Nobody really cares to watch the life experiences of a spoiled sissy with a silver spoon; but we're here for the heroes in The Prince and the Pauper or The Count of Monte Cristo all day long! We like it when the waif becomes a warrior or the cinder girl becomes a queen. What's curious about that popular mindset is that it really isn't fair. Why should someone who was never born to rule get to usurp the throne when those with royal blood in their veins have had to put up with a tedious prim and proper lifestyle of regulations, restrictions, court etiquette and grumpy tutors every day? After all, there is also a price to be paid for being at the top!

Born to Privilege

Is it Fate?

We could discuss the scenarios and the circumstances forever and come up with a plethora of different opinions and solutions, only to find ourselves back at square one: Life is rarely fair, and mostly unpredictable! So let's talk about something we can actually change: our own destinies. Even before I understood how much I had to say about my destiny, I always had an adverse reaction to the age-old axiom, "It's just fate," as if Fate was a neighborhood bully or an evil step-mother waiting in the wings to take over at the slightest vulnerability or difficult set of circumstances. Needless to say, I was excited to discover as I went through life that my future was in my own hands, and not left to Fate unless I handed it over by my own free will! We can say that our lives are in God's hands, of course, because He is the Giver of all life to begin with. We are on dangerous ground, however, if we use either God or Fate (or the neighborhood bully) as an excuse to flounder or flop around with little or no purpose. Along with His beautiful Gift of Life to us, God provided an instruction manual that, if followed, will lead to success and fulfillment; and neither Fate nor "the evil step-mother" will have anything to say about it!

Author and speaker, Charles Swindoll, said, "I am convinced that life is 10% what happens to me and 90% of how I react to it."[3] This plainly blows Fate right out of the water, defining our difficulties as the normal twists and turns of our earthly experience – none of which come as a surprise to God. Therefore, we can go to Him and say, "Now what?" Because He knows exactly what our next steps should be for making the best of every trouble that meets us on the road. We can always choose to think and respond, instead of reacting out of fear or confusion. Please stop saying, "Well, it's just fate. I guess everything happens for a reason." This is blind acceptance of whatever happens to land in front of you; when a better response would be to ponder, "Where did this come from and what can I do about it?" Don't leave anything to Fate! Face your

---

[3] Charles Swindoll, *The Grace Awakening* (Nashville: W Publishing Group, Thomas Nelson, 1990)

obstacles and, with good counsel, *choose* your outcomes. Granted, we sometimes face battles that are too great for us because we have a great enemy who wants the worst for us. Those are the times when we fight on our knees because we know the battle is the Lord's and He will win the victory on our behalf.[4] This is, however, still an "outcome" that we choose – giving it to God when there is little or nothing we can do ourselves.

All that being said, where does our journey begin of "being the best ME that I can be"? The journey begins with the two age-old questions about the meaning of life: *Who am I?* and *Why am I here?* Maybe the rags-to-riches theme isn't fair on the average spectrum of earthly human expectation. But guess who else likes those stories, and especially the rich and happy endings that would otherwise be out of reach? God Himself, our Creator and Giver of Life! Even more amazing —at least from the world's perspective —is God's eternal view that puts all of humanity in the "rags" category anyway! He says that it doesn't matter how much we have or don't have; what we've done, or failed to do; where we've been, or not been; how hard we have worked, or how craftily we have skated through life's obligations—we are all scullery maids and paupers regardless of our journey. Wait! Caution light! Before you get mad at God for looking at us this way, think about it. If we all start out at the same place, isn't that more just and true than the comparisons people often use to define some as having a higher rank than others in life? After all, revisiting our rags-to-riches theme, one of the most thrilling elements of these stories is discovering that the beggar's character is superior to that of the rich man, revealing the pauper as having more wealth than he imagined and the prince as being quite needy after all!

If every vessel starts from a lump of the same clay and the Potter chooses how each one will be used after completion, it removes all the competition and comparison from the equation of purpose. Yet

---

[4] For an excellent discourse on this subject, hear "When the Battle Chooses You", Pastor Steven Furtick, June 2, 2019, https://elevationchurch.org/sermons/when-the-battle-chooses-you/

Born to Privilege

God, in His sovereign wisdom, has designed us, not as pots with no eyes and no voice; but as living, breathing, thinking beings that have a free will and innumerable choices and options before us! Some of the most prominent societal attitudes stem from negativism – always seeing the glass half-empty; fearfulness – being more afraid of everything than hopeful about anything; and self-centeredness – focusing only on what makes one look good, feel good, sound good and win their own game at the expense of everyone else. We don't have to look at life that way just because others do. Our world view can be filled with eagerness and expectation if we have a mindset of fulfillment and success; for, in Christ, we have everything we need for those best outcomes! He has taken the ashes of our lives and has adorned us with heavenly beauty instead. Now we can live by 2 Peter 1:3: *"By his divine power, God has given us everything we need for living a godly life. We have received all of this by coming to know him, the one who called us to himself by means of his marvelous glory and excellence"* (New Living Translation).

So, Who Are You Anyway?

The answer to this question is actually very easy; you don't even have to wonder about it. It was decided by your Creator before you were ever a thought in your mother's mind. Take comfort in hearing this nugget about your personal history from Jeremiah, the prophet. *"I knew you before I formed you in your mother's womb..."* (Jeremiah 1:5 NLT).

Let that sink in... because that truth – all by itself – is enough to thrill your mind and soul with confidence about your destiny. Just pause for a moment and let yourself feel the comfort of those loving arms around you. Somebody who is all-powerful has wrapped you in His everlasting love! Capture this truth and make it a foundational mindset in your brain!

Remember the 1998 movie, <u>Ever After</u>? Danielle, the star of the show played by Drew Barrymore, wasn't always a "commoner".

She started out as a cherished daughter who was the pride and joy of the affluent, Auguste de Barbarac, a *seigneur*, or lord of a large manor and property in 16th century France. She was a little princess loved by all until her well-meaning father, a widower, re-married a baroness with two daughters in an effort to revive a family atmosphere for Danielle to grow up in. Alas, we all know how his sudden death leaves his beloved daughter destitute instead – the help instead of the heiress. Danielle becomes the servant girl to her evil and grasping step-mother; not to mention the object and helpless victim of Baroness de Ghent's vicious jealousy that will stop at nothing to keep her hungry and barefoot.[5]

Bad Seeds, Good Seeds

Nobody wants to focus on that part, as we discussed earlier; but let's talk about it for a moment because it is often a picture of life and circumstance for many women. Can you look back on your early years as a child and remember some bad seeds that spread a dark cloud on what should have been a happy childhood? Whether it was through poverty, or loss, or the selfish actions of another person many of us have felt broken and bruised in our youth. Maybe you had a wonderful childhood, but you married into something you didn't see coming when you joyfully said, "I do" from the innocence of your pearly hopes. You soon discovered through the tear-stained windows of your broken heart that diamonds are not really forever after all. Or, you could be one of those that were good kids from happy homes who actually married securely and raised a happy family; only to watch one of your children make all the choices you hoped they never would. Now you spend lots of time on your knees telling God that you would give up much of your own happiness and success if it would somehow put your young adult on a better plain of experience or give them a hand-up to a purposeful life. You can't; and here's why: God has designed life to be lived individually. No one gets to do family life as a group project where everyone shares the A+

---

[5] "Auguste de Barbarac," Ever After, A Cinderella Story Wiki, Fandom, https://ever-after-cinderella.fandom.com/wiki/Auguste_de_Barbarac

Born to Privilege

work of the best student. Each person is responsible for the elements of their own destiny. Yes, a man and a woman can choose gold for themselves, their marriage and their home life but have a child who chooses lead – heavy and dull, and known for its poisoning capabilities![6]

How can we all live in the same world and end up with such opposite outcomes? Let's talk about perspective. Going back to our <u>Ever After</u> scenario, the prince – who feels trapped by his royal position – is told by his father, the King of France, that he will either cooperate with an arranged marriage to a Spanish princess or lose the prestigious crown of France. Our heroine, Danielle, on the other hand, later encourages Prince Henry that his crown is a privilege that can be used to accomplish great things. Let's look at these two perspectives from opposite sets of circumstances and see what we can draw out of this comparison for our own benefit. What is the crown?

The Queen's Definition is Political and Prejudiced:

- Her Crown is a headdress. She sees it as her claim to supremacy, and its authority protects her position and ensures her control.
- This mindset chooses alliances that expand power and protect personal agendas. It gains personal prosperity at the expense of others.
- This attitude builds a man-made structure that promotes human exploitation, requires competition, and rewards greed.

The Commoner's Definition is Purposeful and Objective:

- Her Crown as a heart attitude. She sees it as a privilege, and its authority uses her position to protect others and create opportunities.

---

[6] "Minerals, Precious Metals, and Gems," Geological Survey, www.gsi.ie/en-ie/geoscience-topics/geology/Pages/Minerals-Precious-Metals-and-Gems.aspx

- This mindset chooses connections to encourage health and success for many. It extends prosperity for others at the expense of personal control.
- This attitude supports a God-given structure that builds upon spiritual principles, rejects competitive thinking, and rewards benevolence and generosity.

It's important to note from these comparisons that both perspectives begin from the same precedent: that the crown is an instrument that comes with authority and responsibility. But we can see that the attitudes of the world will justify perspectives and actions that are self-seeking because they are built on human wisdom. Instead, we need to pursue our destinies in the light of God's Word and the standards that He has set forth for us to live by, which are tough in principle while tender toward our fellow-man.

Tiaras in Spurs

The cover of this book displays a pair of boots with spurs, topped with a glittering tiara, because it is an accurate representation of the "place" we hold in this world as the Daughters of God. The tiara represents the privilege – our position in Christ from Ephesians 2:6, which explains that we are seated with Christ in the heavenly realms and share in His eternal inheritance. The boots with spurs represent the responsibility we have, mainly in two arenas. First, to each other, as taken from our key verse for this study, Hebrews 10:24-25, which reminds us that we must be about the business of encouraging each other continually. Secondly, we have a responsibility to our own life and destiny. When a cowgirl rides a horse she uses her spurs to firmly encourage her reluctant, fearful, or stubborn steed in the right direction. As she and her horse become familiar with each other and secure in their relationship, the horse will eventually sense the direction that the mistress desires it to go, and will need less and less spurring to make the necessary progress. Without encouragement, however, there could be a lot of wasted time floundering around in circles of sweat and dust; and that's how life can be at times. Learning our place and working at

Born to Privilege

the responsibility that comes with it is blending "position" with "purpose", which will eventually create the perfect balance of character for the Women of the Kingdom. This balance is imperative because one without the other will undoubtedly lead to a lop-sided experience somewhere between Calamity Jane[7] and the Princess and the Pea![8] We want to develop the tough as well as the tender, for too much 'tough' might get us a lot of attention while resulting in a bad reputation and very few loyal friends. In our society, women are often encouraged to be brassy, controlling, unfeminine and too careless with their hearts and minds. This is not who we are! Yet neither are we the other extreme of modern societal norms that allows (and even expects) feelings and emotions to rule us and others! God has provided His daughters with a station in life that develops both a tough skin and a tender heart simultaneously!

Like any character strength, these elements can either become a blessing or a burden for us. Remember the Parable of the Talents in Matthew 25? Two of them took what the master gave them and used it for growth and prosperity. Consequently, as the master intended, it became a blessing for them. The fearful one, on the other hand, could think of nothing to do with his talent except hide it in the ground so there would be no chance of his making a mistake with it! His blessing immediately became a burden that caused anxiety for him. He was not commended for this choice when the master returned, but was rather sharply reproved! His talent was taken away and given to another who had accepted the responsibility and considered it a blessing to be counted trustworthy in the master's eyes. We are all given the opportunity to succeed; to make the very best of what we have before us. We can choose life and success, or fear and failure. So don't view your blessing as a burden! The ability to embrace your opportunities stems directly from your understanding of who you are. If you have accepted

---

[7]"Calamity Jane," Biography, July 16, 2019,
https://www.biography.com/performer/calamity-jane
[8] "Princess and the Pea," Wikipedia,
https://en.wikipedia.org/wiki/The_Princess_and_the_Pea

salvation through Jesus Christ and decided to allow Him lordship in your life, this is who you are:

"I, (state your full name), am a daughter of the King. I bear His name, I carry His authority, I radiate His nature, and I am heiress to His riches."

If this is your first opportunity to accept Christ as the Savior and Lord of your life, you will never regret taking the time to do this now. Repeat this prayer aloud, or make a similar confession of your own:

"Thank you, Jesus, for giving your life on the cross to redeem me from the penalty of my own transgressions. I accept your offering of innocent blood that washes me clean from sin and shame. I receive your forgiveness and your gift of New Life. Be my Lord, and forever guide my steps. Amen."

Now that you *know* you are His, please repeat aloud the "King's Daughter Declaration" above!

Chapter One Summary

We have discovered the foundations of who you really are, and reinforced the fact that you have all you need to become the best YOU that you can be! No matter what your beginnings, through Christ you exchanged your ashes for a new and eternal beauty that will never fade. You can anticipate a bright and fulfilling future beginning right now because it is based on your own choices. Tomorrow is the first day of the rest of your life, and if you decide to run with it no one can stop you! No person, entity, circumstance, or obstacle can prevent you from being all that God intended you to be. The decision is all yours, and you can do all things through Christ who strengthens you! (Philippians 4:13) Now it is time to gather your treasures and tools, and then decide what you want to do about it!

Born to Privilege

Theme Verse

Isaiah 61:3 (NLT): *"To all who mourn in Israel, he will give a crown of beauty for ashes, a joyous blessing instead of mourning, festive praise instead of despair. In their righteousness, they will be like great oaks that the LORD has planted for his own glory."*

Take-away Gems

- Friendship is important; I need a Circle of Wagons. (See Preface for description)
- Jesus gave me Beauty for Ashes when I became His.
- I am re-born to privilege through Christ.
- "Tiaras in Spurs" represents my privileged position with its purposeful responsibility.
- I can choose to see my opportunities as either a blessing or a burden; I choose Blessing!
- My confidence in what Christ has given me will enable me to encourage others.
- I can always "wear my tiara", and see life from a Daughter of the King perspective.

Own It!

Personalize: Make a small placard of the "King's Daughter Declaration" found above the *Chapter One Summary*. Decorate it with stars, crowns, gemstones, or other designations of royalty. Stand before a mirror and tell that woman who she is according to the Master of her Destiny! Recite your identity declaration often in order to plant these truths deep in your heart. Think of them throughout the day so you can use them as tools in your everyday life. This will help you to become the kind of vessel that does not only stand tall and confident in your place, but it will enable you to spread light and wealth to others that you come in contact with - in your family, in the church, and in the world.

Ponder: In every chapter of the study, determine to "find a nugget" that you can identify with and use in your own experience. I will highlight a list of "Take-away Gems" at the end of each chapter. I encourage you to get a small journal or notebook and write these down each time. Then jot down your thoughts and questions as you ponder them and think about how each one relates to you personally. Own these gems of truth and progress. They are part of your inheritance!

Pursue: Find a tiara at a Dollar Store, a party store, or even a secondhand shop. This "Born to Privilege" mascot will help you remember how important you are to God. You are seated with Christ in heavenly places, remember? He has great plans for you. Do not feel silly about your crown. This tiara will be our version of a thinking cap for this study. Strong women think deeply about life and about their decisions. Practice engaging your mind with the concepts you are learning; and mentally "wear your tiara" during the day as you face your duties and challenges according to who you are in Christ.

Persist: Write out the theme verse for Chapter One on a 3 x 5 card and tape it to a mirror or the dash of your car; or post it with magnets on the refrigerator or a file cabinet – someplace where you can see it every day! Use the version in the chapter text, or look up the verse in your own Bible and copy it from the Bible version that you prefer. Our theme verses will be the kinds of truths that the Psalmist refers to in Psalm 119:11, *"I have hidden your word in my heart that I might not sin against you"* (NLT). Becoming all that we were created to be includes learning to think like God does; and packing our hearts and minds with His living word is the best place to start!

Partner: Make a list of friends or potential friends, in your current circle of influence (i.e. job, neighborhood, school, church, charity organization or family). Choose a small group of 1-7 individuals that you would like to include in your own Circle of Wagons. These should be women who can identify with at least

Born to Privilege

one element of your personal pathway (i.e. stage of life, faith, marriage status, motherhood, life purpose, pursuits) and whom you would like to share your journey with. Say a prayer that the ones who should be included will be interested and available when you decide to get together.

Chapter 2: Chosen by God

In Chapter One we learned that, no matter what our background or experience, we all get to start at the same Square One with God. No social classes; no "rich kids"; no competition. We are all "clay" that needs to be shaped, polished, and filled by the Master Potter! We stepped down from our "thrones", climbed up from our "hovels", or walked out of our various neighborhood familiarities to see life at a new level – equal with everyone else! Then we recognized 2 Peter 1:3 as the key to a new mindset that we will need to adopt going forward: God has already given us everything that we need for a happy and successful life through our ongoing relationship with Him! We realized that accepting Christ as Lord and Savior changes everything and we declared our new identities as Daughters of the King who—no matter the status of our natural birth – have been re-born to a higher privilege than we thought possible. So, let's get going!

Defining the Privilege

Now that you realize you have traded your "rags" for new riches through Christ Jesus, what's the privilege of your new position? Look at Ephesians 1:3 and 11. *"All praise to God, the Father of our Lord Jesus Christ, who has blessed us with every spiritual blessing in the heavenly realms because we are united with Christ...* [11]*Furthermore, because we are united with Christ, we*

Born to Privilege

have received an inheritance from God, for he chose us in advance, and he makes everything work out according to his plan" (NLT).

First, we are no longer dressed in shame. A quick Old Testament study will show us that ashes were representative of grief, sadness, despair and shame; such as the two stories in Esther 4:1-3 and 2 Samuel 13:18-19. We, on the other hand, have been rescued from all of that and dressed in robes of righteousness (see Isaiah 61:10). Our relationship with Christ comes with what the Bible calls "garments of salvation". This is the spiritual beauty that covers our being when our sins have been washed away and our souls have been cleansed by the power of God. The Righteousness of Christ becomes our clothing, like the gown and jewelry of a princess which identifies her as part of the royal family.

Secondly, we are now citizens of Heaven since we were transferred to the Kingdom of Light at conversion. Colossians 1:11-14 explains: *"We also pray that you will be strengthened with all his glorious power so you will have all the endurance and patience you need. May you be filled with joy, [12] always thanking the Father. He has enabled you to share in the inheritance that belongs to his people, who live in the light. [13] For he has rescued us from the kingdom of darkness and transferred us into the Kingdom of his dear Son, [14] who purchased our freedom and forgave our sins"* (NLT). This is another change of mindset that we need to adopt and review often. We actually belong to a different kingdom! We are children of the light who are no longer prisoners of sin. A rescue operation has taken place, ushering us out of the darkness of a world without God (see Ephesians 2:12) and into a life of eternal hope and peace (see Ephesians 2:4-6). Oh yes; we are still on Earth, walking our human pathways, but at the same time we are part of another realm; the supernatural realm of the spirit where eternal realities take precedence over our finite human existence. We are found, forgiven, and free to succeed with the help and blessing of God. Because we are united with God's Son, we are part of His family and we share in all the privileges that come with having a place in Heaven.

Rebecca Bryan-Howell

Understanding the Responsibility

Remember our theme verse for Chapter One? The end of it says that we will be like great oak trees planted by the Lord for His own glory. I love how the New International Version describes this, *"...a planting of the Lord for the display of his splendor."* God delights in redeeming us and making us new creatures, but the benefits go much farther than saving us out of our troubles and cleaning us up. We are redeemed for the purpose of bringing glory to God. Our lives matter; not just because He loves us and wants to care for us, but because we are ordained for a higher purpose than we could ever come up with on our own. He wants to pour His life through us to the rest of the world! We are honorary vessels that are slated to be used for His glorious and eternal purposes, which go far beyond the wisdom of man or life on this planet! Next time you look in the mirror and recite your King's Daughter Declaration, smile and add, *"I was chosen to display the splendor of the King in all His majesty!"*

In this study, we are learning how to become "the best ME that I can be". However, most of us already know that our "best ME" will include others; because serving someone besides ourselves is the only guarantee that we will not end up with a life full of "Me, Myself, and I"! This poem from my early childhood was always delightful to me. The lyrics sent my active imagination off into magical places to play and pretend!

    Three Guests[9]

    I had a little tea party
    This afternoon at three.
    'Twas very small—

---

[9] Jessica Nelson North, 'Three Guests', in The Poems of Early Childhood/Childcraft, edited by J. Morris Jones (Chicago: Field Enterprises Educational Corporation, 1954) Volume I

Born to Privilege

> Three guests in all—
> Just I, myself and me.
>
> Myself ate all the sandwiches,
> While I drank up the tea;
> 'Twas also I who ate the pie
> And passed the cake to me!

In reality, however, it is more likely an effort to make a lonely child feel better about circumstances they cannot change. Dolls and teddy bears on your picnic blanket are a wonderful way to make the best of being alone, but in the grown up world it is not so simple to imagine loneliness away, because life is meant to be shared. Together we will discover that God has given each of us talents, abilities, personalities, and many gifts; but we will also learn that they have a much higher purpose than our own consumption and personal benefit. They are given so that we might be equipped to accomplish the will of our Creator. In <u>Ever After</u>, Rodmilla de Ghent is continually conniving to get her awful daughter, Marguerite, noticed by royalty in hopes that she can marry the Prince of France and become queen someday, which the evil stepmother sees as her own ticket to Christmas in Paris and a life of portentous self-indulgence. Danielle, the commoner/heroine, who eventually does marry the prince, sees more than the power and profit of her crown; she sees the purpose for the greater good, and considers it a privilege to bless and prosper the people of her realm. Likewise, our own lives must reflect a dedication to God's will and purpose, rather than an allegiance to our personal preferences and selfish ambitions. Our responsibility is to learn what is important to God, and then to pursue those things wholeheartedly – and with the greatest confidence.

Exemplary Women

Two biblical heroines from whom we can learn a great deal are Abigail and Esther. We find the story of Abigail's Intervention in 1 Samuel 25:2-38. In a nutshell, David and his band of warriors had requested provisions from a very wealthy man called Nabal, who also happened to be the ill-tempered drunk-of-a-husband to sweet Abigail! He was rich, rude, and selfish; which explains why he not only refused to accommodate David and his men but also insulted them publically. Abigail was told of the incident and how her foolish husband's behavior had jeopardized the safety of everyone else in his territory. She flew into action and packed up plenty of provisions, which she personally delivered. She hastily rode into the mountain ravine to meet David's army – which by now was on approach to slaughter the entire household – where she humbly presented her generous peace offering with a gracious apology. Her wisdom, foresight, and boldness not only protected her and her household, but also saved the skin of her dimwitted husband – for a few hours at least. When he awoke from his drunken stupor and heard how close he had come to meeting his Maker, he had a stroke and died anyway! Abigail's courage saved her people and made her a princess.

Esther's courage is outlined in the biblical account of the book of Esther, chapter four. When her uncle, Mordecai, discovered an evil plot to annihilate all the Jews in the province of Susa under King Xerxes, he informed Esther who was already queen – a whole separate miracle story. He asked her to act against royal protocol in going before the king uninvited to plead for mercy for the Jews. After fasting and prayer, she did so and was received with gladness by her lord. Esther's courage saved her people and brought swift judgement upon Haman, her accuser and his nation, the Amalekites.

Both of these brave women were confident in their callings and consequently accomplished great things in their time. Look at them with respect and awe if you will, but go to your mirror and look at the lady in front of you as well; for each of you who belong to the Lord were also "born for such a time as this" (Esther 4:14). Since you are making history anyway, let's talk about how to make it in a confident, positive way that will "serve your people" well and leave a legacy for others to follow!

Born to Privilege

Anointed to Serve

Abigail and Esther were great examples of women who used what they had been gifted with for the good of their people and the accomplishment of God's will in their lives and in their slices of human history. You might think that you could never do what they did; but your choices today are just as powerful to effect change in your life and in your world as theirs were long ago! Yes, it's a choice and they made the right ones; so can you. Even Jesus, our ultimate example of giving everything for the eternal purposes of God, had to make the choice to do it. He offered Himself of His own free will, and this is the opportunity that each of us has been given. Psalm 139 is an awesome prayer that acknowledges God's sovereignty in the lives of those who belong to Him. It reminds us that God knows everything about us, even our thoughts, and sees our actions before we do them. He is before us and behind us to guide and protect; we can never escape from His Spirit, for He is ever-present. He made us lovingly and with purpose; and His thoughts about us are tender and kind. He is the Potter and we are His valuable workmanship. Verse 16 of this chapter reads, *"You saw me before I was born. Every day of my life was recorded in your book. Every moment was laid out before a single day had passed"* (NLT). Do you understand the implications of that? We are safe and significant! Your destiny is very secure!

We can pause for practicality's sake and toss in a caveat: free will. Naturally, the lump of clay that stays on the wheel is much more likely to become a beautiful, useable finished product than the lump that keeps jumping off to investigate its other options (like bruises, bumps, and broken pieces from hitting the deck again and again!) In addition, no matter how we work to choose the best course, life often surprises us with the unexpected obstacle or the disagreeable relationship that adds pain and/or misery to our pathway. Not to mention our arch enemy who will stop at nothing to get us off-track or discouraged. Yet I can tell you with unwavering surety that nothing takes God by surprise and, despite our individual ups and downs, His part of the trust is solid and He has answers and help for all the rest. You can do anything that God wants you to do! Look at Abraham and Sarah. They were too old to have children, but because Isaac was God's will and they were the chosen vessels, and willing to cooperate, no human limitation could prevent it. God reminds us all through our lives that nothing is too hard for Him! So let's determine in our own hearts that we are chosen by God, anointed for His service, and able to do all that He asks of us! Additionally, and equally important, let's remember to encourage each other in the same way.

Chapter Two Summary

This lesson helped us to see that there is much more to our "re-born to privilege" status than having our sins forgiven and all shame removed. It means that we have been transferred to the Kingdom of Light where we are citizens who share in the heavenly inheritance of Christ Jesus! We found out that this spiritual reality coincides with our earthly pilgrimage to empower us and strengthen our journey in the earthly realm while preparing us for our eternal destiny as well. We learned that being chosen by God means allowing Him to enable us for doing His work with the gifts and abilities He has given us. We now understand that we were created to display His splendor; and when we live according to God's plan, our destinies are secure. Like Esther and Abigail, our choices are powerful and we can be confident in doing anything that God wants us to do. We were born just at the right time for our lives to glorify God and encourage others along the way.

Theme Verse

Ephesians 1:11 (NLT): *"Furthermore, because we are united with Christ, we have received an inheritance from God, for he chose us in advance, and he makes everything work out according to his plan."*

Born to Privilege

Take-away Gems

- I have been chosen by God.
- I belong to the Kingdom of Light.
- I am dressed in royal robes – the Righteousness of Christ.
- I am seated in the heavenly realms with Jesus, even while walking this earth.
- God is working through me to accomplish His eternal will.
- I was born to fulfill a purpose greater than my own ambitions.
- My destiny is safe and secure.
- I can do all things through Christ, who is my strength.

Own It!

Personalize: Recite the King's Daughter Declaration several times this week to get these five truths planted deeply in the new mindset that you are developing through this study. At least one of these times, repeat this recitation standing in front of a mirror to foster a healthy say-hear-see connection in your brain about who you are in Christ. Put on your tiara and enjoy it – no shame!

Ponder: If you don't already have some time to yourself periodically, find a slot that you can designate each week for personal reflection. Write down the Take-away Gems for Chapter Two in your journal and choose one that you most identify with. Write something about how you identify with it, how it encourages you, or what you will do to activate this truth in your heart. You may also choose a different nugget that you found while reading this chapter, and write about that instead. Own all of your gems of truth and progress. They are part of your inheritance!

Pursue: As an act of devotion, place a drop of oil on your forehead, such as olive oil, frankincense, or others you may have on hand. Let the oil represent the anointing of the Holy Spirit upon your life and pray this prayer, or your own prayer, of dedication to God.

Lord Jesus, I receive this token of your anointing upon my life. I accept that you have truly chosen me, and I believe that I can do anything you want me to do. I trust your Holy Spirit to work within my heart and teach me your ways. Thank you for making me a vessel of your light and truth. Help me to honor you all the days of my life. Give me the wisdom to make strong choices, and the words to encourage others along my pathway. Amen to your perfect will.

Persist: Write out the theme verse for Chapter Two on a 3 x 5 card in the Bible version of your choice. Tape it to a mirror or the dash of your car; or post it with magnets on the refrigerator or a file cabinet – wherever you can see it often! Remember that hiding these verses in your heart and reviewing them in your mind will help you to learn to think like God does. Bringing your thoughts in line with the mind of Christ will enable you to become all that you were created to be!

Partner: Gather your partners group, or at least meet with one friend if you haven't formed your Circle of Wagons, yet. (If you need a reminder about this important concept, see the Take-away Gems for Chapter One.) Talk about each of the five truths in the King's Daughter Declaration. Share any that are hard for you to accept or identify with and discuss why. Pray together about them and ask God to strengthen your hearts and to increase your confidence about who you are in Christ.

Chapter 3: Called Out: A Patent for Purpose

In Chapter Two we began to define "the privilege" that came with our "spiritual birth" into the Kingdom of Light. We talked about the far-reaching benefits of our redemption, and about why our lives matter so much more than we thought they did! We addressed a main purpose of this study: "Becoming the best ME that I can be", and reviewed the vital concept of relationship with others in preventing our lives from becoming in-grown and self-centered. We learned that we were created for God's purpose, meaning that we have a responsibility to learn what is important to Him and pursue it wholeheartedly. Abigail and Esther were biblical heroines whose examples we were given for us to emulate, since our choices are making history today just as their choices made history in their times. Similarly, we realized that when we are faithful to God we are able to accomplish whatever He sets before us to do. So, what is it? And what's this "patented" theme in our title for Chapter Three?

Called out of What?

Well...the world! No worries, ladies, this is not about an alien abduction or wild conspiracy theory! Remember in Chapter Two when we discussed our transfer to the Kingdom of Light? It may sound a bit spooky at first to think of yourself walking in two realms at the same time, but get used to it because you were created for eternity! We are three-part beings: body, soul and spirit. Your

Born to Privilege

body will die someday, just as everything else on this earth grows old, decays, and dies. It is simply a temporary house for your soul and spirit; but your spirit lives forever! It is the part of you that communicates with God, your Creator, and interacts with that "supernatural realm of the spirit" where eternal realities take precedence over our finite human existence. At this point in your destiny, however, you are walking the part of your pathway that winds through this tangible, earthly habitat along with all the other physical life-forms that God made when He created the amazing world we live in. We all understand that Earth is a temporary location because we know that human life does not last forever; but our study affirms that the spiritual re-birth we talked about earlier came with the promise of a whole "New Life" that would change our destiny completely! When we chose Christ as Lord, we were separated from the world. A dictionary definition of the word, *separate*, would include the action of keeping apart or dividing by a barrier or space. It's an intervention that forces something away from something else; or in relationships, to part company or withdraw from personal association.[10]

Picture a vessel removed from a pile of rubble and placed on a shelf: worn, but unique; used, but full of potential; cracked, but salvageable. That's us! When God rescued us, we were removed from a place where we could be broken, contaminated, abused and ignored; and we were placed in God's keeping for His renovation process. Have you seen the popular home and garden shows where the right artist or craftsman takes a run-down property and creates something beautiful? That's us again! God is our Master Craftsman who makes us new and sets us apart for His eternal purposes. Let's look at our biblical precedents for being set apart.

In The Old Testament we learn that God physically separated Israel from heathen nations. *"But as for you, the LORD took you and brought you out of the iron-smelting furnace, out of Egypt, to be the*

---

[10] Dictionary.com, https://www.dictionary.com/browse/separate

people of his inheritance, as you now are" (Deuteronomy 4:20 NIV).

They were being abused! Exodus 6:6 tells us, *"Therefore, say to the Israelites: 'I am the LORD, and I will bring you out from under the yoke of the Egyptians. I will free you from being slaves to them, and I will redeem you with an outstretched arm and with mighty acts of judgment"* (NIV). He was displeased about their conditions and offered them freedom from bondage.

They were not only slaves, though; they were also being tarnished and contaminated, as we read in Leviticus 20:23-24 *"Do not live according to the customs of the people I am driving out before you. It is because they do these shameful things that I detest them. ^{24}But I have promised you, 'You will possess their land because I will give it to you as your possession—a land flowing with milk and honey.' I am the LORD your God, who has set you apart from all other people"* (NLT). God had a better destiny for His people than Egypt could provide; and the same is true for us today.

God calls us out of the world for the same reasons. *"But you are not like that, for you are a chosen people. You are royal priests, a holy nation, God's very own possession. As a result, you can show others the goodness of God, for he called you out of the darkness into his wonderful light"* (I Peter 2:9 NLT). We were slaves to sin just as Israel was in bondage to Egypt. Romans 6:6-7 reminds us that when we identify with Christ's death on the cross and receive it as His sacrifice for our sins, we are set free because sin loses its power over us! A world without God will tarnish and corrupt our souls – our minds, our free wills, and our emotions – because it does not honor His sovereignty, His commandments, or His purpose for mankind. That's why we are warned against becoming attached to this world and its influences. *"Do not love this world nor the things it offers you, for when you love the world, you do not have the love of the Father in you. ^{16}For the world offers only a craving for physical pleasure, a craving for everything we see, and pride in our achievements and possessions. These are not from the*

Born to Privilege

Father, but are from this world. ^{17}*And this world is fading away, along with everything that people crave. But anyone who does what pleases God will live forever"* (I John 2:15-17 NLT). As the old song says, "All that glitters is not gold!"

The Artist's Signature

Let's talk about our "patent". A patent is not restricted to the exclusive right to sell something; it's a protection of identity and proof of ownership. When God calls us out of the world He puts His signature of ownership on our lives! He is telling the world that we belong to Him and that we are a part of His eternal purpose! As we learn to walk in His ways, His light begins to shine from our lives and people notice! Genesis 41:37-44 and Daniel 1:17-20 record parts of the remarkable lives of two great Bible heroes, Joseph and Daniel. In reading these passages, we can easily pick out the symbols of supernatural favor that caused them to stand out in the heathen cultures that surrounded them. We can find the supreme brand of the God of Israel all over these two men throughout these passages. They were well-received; noticeably resonant with the spirit of God; possessed higher levels of intelligence, deeper wisdom, unusual aptitudes, and special abilities. Not to mention the fine clothing, gold chains and signet rings they wore to represent their positions of prominence in these regimes! Yet none of these things were the results of human competition, climbing the social ladder, or pure luck. These were all marks of God's favor on their lives, and evidence of the higher purposes that he had ordained for each of them to fulfill during their lifetimes. Why compete with the world systems of dog-eat-dog and keeping-up-with-the-Jones's when we can have supernatural favor instead? Frequently our work places, social groups, and even family atmospheres can be dominated by the ignoble mentality of climbing over others to get to the top, often ending with no real fame and few loyal friends! Come, ladies; we have a higher identity to claim! As God's daughters we are indeed patented for purpose; lovingly etched with the signature of the Almighty who delights in protecting each of our destinies as a heartfelt quest of His very own.

When our surrounding cultures look at us, what are the marks that they see distinguishing us as people set apart by God? The world is not completely ignorant about what God looks like, after all! Have you ever had co-workers apologize for their swearing or dirty jokes before you ever revealed your faith to them? How about meeting a new friend in your neighborhood or community group and finding that you share the same faith, only to have them exclaim, "I thought for sure you must be a Christian!" Jesus shines to the world; and when we belong to Him that light shines through us. The Bible is very clear about the marks or characteristics that define Christianity, and the first one is love. John 13:34-35 reminds us that our love for one another will prove to the world that we are His disciples. 2 Peter 1:3-4 says that God's divine nature dwells within us and is to be shared, or seen, in our lives. We are actually challenged by Matthew 5:14-16 to remember that we are the light of the world! How? Christ, the Light of the World, lives within us and His nature shines out of us to those we interact with. We are to be like a city on a hilltop that can't be hidden! This passage basically asked the question, "Why would you light a lamp and then cover it under a basket? A light must be placed on a post where others can benefit by it!" This means that our choices will line up with God's Word and our deeds will give others a path to follow. Most importantly, the greatest mark of our identity in Christ is the ongoing development of a godly mindset. Having the mind of Christ – being able to think like God does about life and about people – is the crowning quality that fosters all the other features of God's signature on our lives. Because when we think like He does our nature, our love, our light and our deeds will automatically imitate His. If you put a drop of red food coloring in a glass of water, the water cannot be separated from the red! It is no longer described as "water"; now it is "red water". The same is true when we allow the Lord to fill our lives; we will not be separated from Him. We will be one with Him, just as the water becomes one with the red coloring. We are no longer just girls; we are God's girls!

Born to Privilege

Romans 12:2 explains, *"Don't copy the behavior and customs of this world, but let God transform you into a new person by changing the way you think. Then you will learn to know God's will for you, which is good and pleasing and perfect"* (NLT).

Seal of Authority

There is power in belonging to Christ! We begin to recognize that we are not our own, as 1 Corinthians 6:19-20 teaches. Our bodies are now temples of the Holy Spirit because God Himself purchased us at a very high price – the life-blood of His only Son! This means that the life of God in us enables us to fulfill our commission and accomplish our purpose here. The in-filling of the Holy Spirit is the first installment that guarantees everything God has promised us! (2 Corinthians 1:21-22) When Jesus told His disciples that He would soon return to His Father in heaven, they were sad because they couldn't imagine life without Him. He explained to them that when He left this world He would send The Comforter, which was the Holy Spirit, to be their constant teacher and guide through life. They were instructed to wait for this promise, which is the phenomenal biblical account of Acts, chapter two. This was the same Holy Spirit that rested on Jesus at His water baptism when He was anointed for His earthly ministry; and it is the same power He spoke of in The Great Commission of Mark 16:15-18. Jesus sent the same Holy Spirit to fill our lives whom He had in His own miraculous, powerful life on earth prior to His ascension! He has given us access to all the power we need to do His work on earth and to overcome every obstacle!

The power of the Holy Spirit is also a thick layer of supernatural protection against spiritual contamination, which will come at us from a variety of different sources. Even in fairly healthy atmospheres we can encounter folks with a variety of spiritual perspectives, which are determined by their personal levels of experience and understanding. Wherever we are, we will make choices about what we listen to, what we participate in, and what we decide to accept or reject from the plethora of influences around us. Do you have a deck, porch or patio? Have you placed flower pots, outdoor furniture, pillows or candles in these areas to enhance your spaces only to discover that, relatively soon, they become dusty and spotted? In the same way, we are always vulnerable to the dust of the world; even if we consciously stay away from the mud holes! 2 Corinthians 6:14-17 describes the incompatibility of a worldly lifestyle with our life of faith. *"Don't team up with those who are unbelievers. How can righteousness be a partner with wickedness? How can light live with darkness? [15]What harmony can there be between Christ and the devil? How can a believer be a partner with an unbeliever? [16]And what union can there be between God's temple and idols? For we are the temple of the living God...[17]Therefore, come out from among unbelievers, and separate yourselves from them, says the LORD..."* (NLT)

This is why it is imperative, as we take on our new identity in Christ, to dump everything from our old routines, preferences, habits, and associations that might open the door to the sludge and grime that we've been freed from! Even when we dump the old lifestyle, we have to regularly give our lives a good dusting through prayer, Bible study and the fellowship of other believers. *Dump and Dust* has to become a new motto for living in order to "radiate His nature", as our King's Daughter Declaration proclaims. Just living in this world gets us "dusty"; we can't get completely away from it but we don't have to live in it, either! My favorite scripture for handling the dust and grime of the world is Psalm 51:10; and nobody says it like the King James Version: *"Create in me a clean heart, O God, and renew a right spirit within me."* And He does it faithfully, whenever we ask Him! We can develop a good habit of making this verse a daily and heartfelt prayer. Asking God to cleanse our minds and hearts each night of any "stinking thinking", or negative attitudes we picked up while navigating through our day, is just as imperative for our spiritual health as taking a shower is important for our physical health! What soap and water do for the body, prayer and biblical meditation will do for the soul and spirit. There is never a good reason to "go to bed with dirty feet" because of where we walked that day; for though we may have to

Born to Privilege

"rough it" at times regarding our access to bathing facilities in the natural, we can always be clean spiritually. This is possible because we can never be separated from our access to God, His loving care, or His listening ear when we pray. His promise in Hebrews 13:5 to never leave us, nor forsake us, is true; we do not tread our pathways alone. There will never be a time when we cannot call upon the name of Jesus for help, comfort, cleansing or safety. Indeed, Proverbs 18:10 instructs us that, *"The name of the LORD is a strong fortress; the godly run to him and are safe"* (NLT).

Your Safe Place

Protected things are treated with special care, kept in a safe place, and preserved for special use and purpose. Under God's divine protection, His children are kept in His care like Grandma's china was savored for the holidays. If you compare paper plates, microwavable plastic, and fine china you know that one is disposable, one is re-useable but low quality, and one is expensive, of high quality, and irreplaceable. We are the china in God's household; beautiful vessels of quality that He cherishes and protects for His special purpose. Examples in Scripture show us how Joseph's life was spared, even though he was sold to the Ishmaelites; and his future was protected, even though he was unjustly sentenced to prison for a season. Daniel's enemies set traps for him, but God controlled the outcomes. In both cases, God's perfect plan was ultimately revealed through circumstances that neither of these men could have imagined as being necessary for their success! Yet, their faith in God enabled them to wait and pray, instead of reacting and losing hope because they both knew who they really were, no matter what other people said or did. They were on the Potter's Wheel being formed and polished for God's glory and, however grave their situations looked at times, they enjoyed divine protection through it all!

Each of us has the same opportunity to build our faith, resist our fears, honor our position, accept our purpose and reap the benefits!

The more we practice the spiritual mindset of who we are in Christ, the more benefits we will see in our position, and the more blessing we will gain from our responsibility. Learning to live confidently in a dusty world by safe-guarding our place in the Kingdom of Light with wise decisions and thoughtful actions will go a long ways in "growing" us up into Daughters of the King who radiate His nature and bear the unmistakable marks of His name and His authority in our lives.

Chapter Three Summary

In this chapter we learned that the very world we were born into includes elements that will contaminate us and thwart our destiny if we do not walk carefully. We found that, as citizens of God's eternal kingdom, we have been called out of the world's way of doing life and commissioned to a life that is dictated by the mind of Christ. We saw how God has etched upon our lives His own signature of ownership; and that these distinguishing characteristics are meant to be seen by others as a light on their pathway also. We are set apart by God for a higher destiny than the world can offer. We have actually been "patented for purpose" and the seal of God that we bear comes with all the power and protection we need to navigate through this life with confidence, safety, and success.

Theme Verse

I Peter 2:9 (NLT): *"But you are not like that, for you are a chosen people. You are royal priests, a holy nation, God's very own possession. As a result, you can show others the goodness of God, for he called you out of the darkness into his wonderful light."*

Take-away Gems

- ♦ I have been intentionally set apart by the master of the universe.
- ♦ I am God's special possession.
- ♦ I am marked by the signature of the Almighty.

Born to Privilege

- God's deposit of his Holy Spirit within me guarantees all His promises.
- I am the Temple of the Living God and I have no harmony with darkness.
- Because I have God's favor on my life, I don't need to compete for a place in this world.
- I have constant access to the cleansing power of Christ for spiritual health.
- The mind of Christ – thinking like God does – will give me confidence, safety and success.

Own It!

Personalize: What does "called out" mean in your own life? List some old habits that you have "dumped" since you gave your life to Christ.

Ponder: Are there any associations with the world that you realize are not healthy for a Daughter of God? During your quiet time ask the Holy Spirit to show you areas of your life that still have one foot in the world: relationships, habits, entertainment, words, actions, etc. Write them down and decide what you can do to separate yourself from these worldly influences and ask the Lord Jesus to help you do it.

Pursue: Write down your take-away gems for Chapter Three in your journal or notebook. Which one is most significant for you right now, and why? Talk to a mentor, pastor or Bible teacher about the things you thought through in the section above. Ask them questions about any areas of separation from the world you think you may need to work on or need help understanding.

Persist: Write out the theme verse for Chapter Two on a 3 x 5 card in the Bible version of your choice. Post it wherever you can see it often! Remember that hiding these verses in your heart and reviewing them in your mind will help you to learn to think like

God does. Bringing your thoughts in line with the mind of Christ will enable you to become all that you were created to be!

Partner: In your Circle of Wagons, share the "marks of godly character" you have seen on each other. Let each person share one element of the signature of God that she would like to have in her life and pray together for God to develop these in you for His glory and purpose.

Chapter 4: Charm School

Chapter Three revealed the strategic balance of living in this world while developing our spiritual walk as citizens of God's eternal kingdom. Now that we know there is a way to do both at the same time, we need to gather the tools to cultivate skills for doing life God's way. There is no better way to develop the mind of Christ than to become familiar with the book He gave us to live by – the Bible – and to practice the disciplines of a godly lifestyle. This begins with a mindset of gratitude; recognizing how privileged we are as Daughters of God. Mindsets are developed through capturing our thoughts during times of reflection and analyzing them to determine their source. If our perspectives, of ourselves or others, are tainted by bad experiences and wrong values we need to renew our minds! When we realize that we are struggling to see ourselves as chosen vessels etched with the signature of God, we need to commit to the process of unraveling the lies of our past and replacing them with the truths that will direct our God-ordained destiny. We must recognize that we are being robbed! Jesus told us in the record of His words found in John 10:10, *"The thief's purpose is to steal and kill and destroy. My purpose is to give them a rich and satisfying life"* (NLT). Do you want that rich and satisfying life that the Good Shepherd promises His children? I do! Life is an education, and many of us have adopted the popular phrase "live and learn"[11]; but how we live and what we learn is up

---

[11] Washington Gladden, "Live and Learn", (New York, The Macmillan Company, September, 1914)

to each of us individually! If we are unwilling to learn from our mistakes, or our history, we will keep getting the same negative outcomes. Furthermore, if our sources are from worldly associations, secular philosophies, degrading activities, chaotic family life and the like, we need to go back to school! Let's look at two big words that everybody needs to understand for the good life.

Education and Preparation

Now, don't get hung up on the concept of education – especially if you feel that you have not had the same opportunity as others have for learning – because the world's version of knowledge and truth is not what we're talking about! Although most of our institutions of higher learning began as religious establishments, they are very different today. An article on Forbes.com from 2016 says, "In the beginning, most universities in the U.S. were established as institutions of faith: the colonial colleges – such as Harvard, Yale and Dartmouth (Puritan), College of William and Mary (Church of England), Princeton (Presbyterian) and Rutgers University (Dutch Reformed Church) – were Christian schools in mission or affiliation."[12] These days, however, it is common to hear college professors express in various ways that higher education is not about truth or learning, but about expanding one's horizons and broadening one's views. Dictionaries will define Psychology as the science or study of the mind and behavior. Yet 50% of Psychology professors are atheists, and over 48% of all U.S. professors say that the Bible is an ancient book of fables, according to a study of American college and university professors in 2011.[13] What a disturbing datum, that much of intelligentsia does not believe in "truth with a capital T", when the fact is that God's truth is not only inerrant, but eternal. The philosophies that drive modern society

---

[12] Carter Coudriot, "Top 25 Christian Colleges: The Essential Questions On Religion And Education," Forbes.com, July 19, 2016,
https://www.forbes.com/sites/cartercoudriet/2016/07/19/top-25-christian-colleges-the-essential-questions-on-religion-and-education/#76a6cb2a5576
[13] Amarnath Amarasingam, "Are American College Professors Religious?" HUFFPOST, updated May 25, 2011, https://www.huffpost.com/entry/how-religious-are-america_b_749630

teach that "everything is relative" and what is true for some is not true for all. If we are talking about sports, it may be true that baseball is Gene's favorite, but untrue for Jake since his favorite is basketball. Yet there are principal Truths that cannot be compromised by preference or opinion, such as those found in God's Holy Word; and these are the truths that build solid foundations for a life of joy and fulfillment. God talks about the "world's knowledge" that puffs up the human ego, and His Word reminds us in 1 Corinthians 3:18-19 that the wisdom of this world is not only foolishness to God, but it becomes a trap to those who pursue it.

Anyone who has been a Christian for a while has either heard or experienced the voices of disdain and mockery toward our faith which are so prevalent in today's society. Yet here is what God says about it: *"The message of the cross is foolish to those who are headed for destruction! But we who are being saved know it is the very power of God. [19] As the Scriptures say, 'I will destroy the wisdom of the wise and discard the intelligence of the intelligent.' [20] So where does this leave the philosophers, the scholars, and the world's brilliant debaters? God has made the wisdom of this world look foolish. [21] Since God in his wisdom saw to it that the world would never know him through human wisdom, he has used our foolish preaching to save those who believe"* (1 Corinthians 1:18-21 NLT).

In this day of information overload, due to technological advancements that have brought the greatest libraries into our living rooms, we could dedicate our entire lives to learning and never know the right stuff. The Bible warns that we can gain the whole world and still lose our own soul! *"And what do you benefit if you gain the whole world but lose your own soul? Is anything worth more than your soul?"* (Matthew 16:26 NLT) We need to understand clearly that the wisdom of man is flawed and can never lead us to God. Humans are finite, created beings whose knowledge and understanding are very limited. But the good news is that, as Daughters of the Most High, our knowledge and

Born to Privilege

understanding are not restricted to what the world has to offer. In fact, we have a free-ride scholarship to the best school with personal tutoring by the greatest teacher that ever lived!

The School of the Spirit

Welcome to the School of the Spirit; free of charge and available to all! Your Creator wrote the textbook with your perfect destiny in mind. His comprehensive curriculum will equip anyone for everything. Individual students at all levels of experience and learning can expect:

- The best possible outcomes for life: *"All Scripture is inspired by God and is useful to teach us what is true and to make us realize what is wrong in our lives. It corrects us when we are wrong and teaches us to do what is right. ^{17}God uses it to prepare and equip his people to do every good work"* (2 Timothy 3:16-17 NLT).

- The brightest of futures: *"Your word is a lamp for my feet, a light on my path"* (Psalm 119:105 NIV).

- Flawless teaching: *"The law of the Lord is perfect, refreshing the soul. The statutes of the Lord are trustworthy, making wise the simple. ^{8}The precepts of the Lord are right, giving joy to the heart. The commands of the Lord are radiant, giving light to the eyes. ^{9}The fear of the Lord is pure, enduring forever. The decrees of the Lord are firm, and all of them are righteous. ^{10}They are more precious than gold, than much pure gold; they are sweeter than honey, than honey from the honeycomb. ^{11}By them your servant is warned; in keeping them there is great reward"* (Psalm 19:7-11 NIV).

- Incentives and Rewards: *"Instruct the wise, and they will be even wiser. Teach the righteous, and they will learn even more. ^{10}Fear of the LORD is the foundation of wisdom.*

Knowledge of the Holy One results in good judgment. ¹¹Wisdom will multiply your days and add years to your life. ¹²If you become wise, you will be the one to benefit. If you scorn wisdom, you will be the one to suffer" (Proverbs 9:9-12 NLT).

- Everything needed for the Good Life: *"By his divine power, God has given us everything we need for living a godly life. We have received all of this by coming to know him, the one who called us to himself by means of his marvelous glory and excellence"* (2 Peter 1:3 NLT).

Charm School: Spiritual Etiquette

In the old days, young women of the late 1800s through the middle of the 20th century coveted the opportunity to attend a "finishing school" as they were called in Europe. These establishments provided young women with training in the social graces, etiquette, grooming, and deportment.[14] These schools were considered a great privilege, and they supplied the finishing touch on a young woman's education that prepared her for life in the outside world, especially since many of them were "protected" from outside influence and often encouraged to stay home practicing domestic and nurturing skills until marriage. These classes were labeled "Charm School" in America but were probably expensive, and likely lost their appeal during the world wars and The Great Depression. Certainly, by the 1960s, the movement against high society was wont to pull down everything that smacked of the social classes – upper, middle, and lower – in order to promote commonality and communal living philosophies that tossed everyone into the same pot to share and share alike, or give equal parts to all. That era also brought about a full-fledged rebellion against all authority, throwing out the baby with the bathwater in their efforts to gain personal freedom. This counter-culture chose

---

[14] "Finishing School," Wikipedia, https://en.wikipedia.org/wiki/Finishing_school

Born to Privilege

to drop out of conventional society, or to change it through human attempts that brought more riots and wars.

We all know, especially after our previous discussion about the flawed wisdom of the world, that no form of human intervention be it a finishing school, a university, or a war against the status quo can charm, perfect, or redeem the human race! In fact, going back to Chapter One and our rags-to-riches scenarios, we remember that in God's eyes we are all from the same lump of human clay and every one of us needs the skillful hands of the Master Potter to shape and form our lives into something beautiful, regardless of where we have already been. Romans 3:22-24 says it best; *"We are made right with God by placing our faith in Jesus Christ. And this is true for everyone who believes, no matter who we are. ^{23}For everyone has sinned; we all fall short of God's glorious standard. ^{24}Yet God, in his grace, freely makes us right in his sight. He did this through Christ Jesus when he freed us from the penalty for our sins"* (NLT). How, then, do we get from "saved out of darkness" to "walking in the light"? Well, it's a journey that God has prepared for us by orchestrating each step of our path so we will not slip or get lost along the way. I hope you chose the verse from 2 Peter 1:3 as one of your "nuggets" because it confirms that once you have put your trust in Christ, He gives you *everything* you need to live a godly life that pleases Him and makes you heiress to His riches! It's a big decision to enroll in this progressive and trustworthy learning program. So, let's take a look at some of the courses available for you in the School of the Spirit.

One is The Fruit of the Spirit from Galatians 5:22-25: *"But the Holy Spirit produces this kind of fruit in our lives: love, joy, peace, patience, kindness, goodness, faithfulness, ^{23}gentleness, and self-control. There is no law against these things! ^{24}Those who belong to Christ Jesus have nailed the passions and desires of their sinful nature to his cross and crucified them there. ^{25}Since we are living by the Spirit, let us follow the Spirit's leading in every part of our lives"* (NLT). This course teaches us about the kind of fruit that grows in our lives as we become trees of righteousness. These things are not just a show that can be put on because we learned how to smile for the cameras in charm school. These are living, breathing, elements of the nature of Christ that continue to enrich our lives as we follow in His ways. Fruit trees in the natural world produce only seasonally, but the fruit of the Spirit produces continually.

We talked about the mind of Christ, which is allowing God to work in us to enable us to think like God does about life, people, and purpose. Courses about the Spiritual Mindset will teach us Christ-like behavior as we learn to refuse the influences of the world and to apply the instruction of the Holy Spirit in our daily lives. *"Those who are dominated by the sinful nature think about sinful things, but those who are controlled by the Holy Spirit think about things that please the Spirit. ^{6}So letting your sinful nature control your mind leads to death. But letting the Spirit control your mind leads to life and peace. ^{7}For the sinful nature is always hostile to God. It never did obey God's laws, and it never will"* (Romans 8:5-7 NLT).

Since the Holy Bible is God's manual for Life, there is nothing left out. From building strong relationships, to weathering storms, to developing strong families, careers, or skill sets; it's in the book! Give Him your heart, and He will give you everything you will ever need for success.

Do you remember the terrible stress and dread associated with exams in school? *Did I study the right things? Did I study enough? Did I really learn anything at all this semester? Will I be able to remember the important stuff for the test? What is the important stuff, anyway? Will I fail, and have to re-take this class after all this time?* Don't fret! God is patient, and you can grow and learn at your own pace. Since it is God's will for all of us to "pass", He will help us grow and thrive at every level. We can choose to pursue Him fast and furious, slow and steady, careful and contemplative, or with a learning regimen prepared on our own or by a spiritual mentor. There is freedom here! No pressure to perform. We are changed day by day, learning and growing with every experience, one step at a time. *"For the Lord is the Spirit, and wherever the Spirit of the Lord is, there is freedom. [18]So all of us who have had that veil removed can see and reflect the glory of the Lord. And the Lord—who is the Spirit—makes us more and more like him as we are changed into his glorious image"* (2 Corinthians 3:17-18 NLT).

Practicum: the Spiritual Internship

Internships are short-term periods of temporary work experience for students or trainees, typically lasting for a few weeks or months, and often without pay. The Body of Christ is the best internship for gaining valuable experience and knowledge about the Christian life. Working among other Christians, especially in the church, helps us to learn a lot about people and to gain a working knowledge of "kingdom business". It can also be a valuable course in recognizing our natural strengths and an opportunity to develop our spiritual gifts. When I worked at a local university years ago, our students eagerly applied for any available internship in their fields of study. They not only valued the free education they would gain there, but the additional contacts and opportunities they might find through networking. The Body of Christ works the same way. *"Just as our bodies have many parts and each part has a special function, [5]so it is with Christ's body. We are many parts of one body, and we all belong to each other. [6]In his grace, God has given us different gifts for doing certain things well. So if God has given you the ability to prophesy, speak out with as much faith as God has given you. [7]If your gift is serving others, serve them well. If you are a teacher, teach well. [8]If your gift is to encourage others, be encouraging. If it is giving, give generously. If God has given you leadership ability, take the responsibility seriously. And if you have a gift for showing kindness to others, do it gladly"* (Romans 12:4-8 NLT). One thing we can be sure of is that when we offer our gifts and talents to the work of the Kingdom, our assignments will always enrich our lives and bring out the best in us!

Rebecca Bryan-Howell

Requirements and Continuing Education

Even in the School of the Spirit, there are requirements for progress and achievement. In my job, I advised students of the course requirements they needed in order to graduate with the degree of their choice. Not one of them said, "Yes, I want a degree in Physical Engineering; but I want to take courses in kayaking and photography to get there." They knew at the outset that they had to meet certain requirements in order to reach their goal. Practically speaking, any achievement requires some work! If you want friends, you are required to be friendly. If you want money, you are required to find a job that pays, *and* to set money aside in a savings account. If you want to be physically fit, you are required to follow an exercise program that builds muscle and sheds fat. And if you want to remain healthy, you are required to develop life habits that are good for your body and your brain. So it should not come as a surprise that God has requirements as well; and these things are embedded in that "truth with a capital T" that we talked about earlier. The world touts the philosophy that there are many ways to God, and promotes a plethora of religions – old and new – for people to choose from like a rack of shoes to satisfy a whim. The Truth, however, is that salvation through Jesus Christ is the only way to God. *"Salvation is found in no one else, for there is no other name under heaven given to mankind by which we must be saved"* (Acts 4:12 NIV).

Then, once we have given our hearts to Him, God gives us the steps He has already put in place that are *necessary* to build our faith and keep us spiritually strong. *"For there is one body and one Spirit, just as you have been called to one glorious hope for the future. [5]There is one Lord, one faith, one baptism, [6]and one God and Father, who is over all and in all and living through all"* (Ephesians 4:4-6 NLT). Additionally, there is always more to learn and farther to grow; because our "continuing education program" is our relationship with Christ! When we walk with Him and commune with Him through His Word and through the Holy Spirit,

Born to Privilege

our teacher and guide, we have everything we will ever need as these vital scriptures declare:

"I want them to be encouraged and knit together by strong ties of love. I want them to have complete confidence that they understand God's mysterious plan, which is Christ himself. ³In him lie hidden all the treasures of wisdom and knowledge" (Colossians 2:2-3 NLT).

"What we have received is not the spirit of the world, but the Spirit who is from God, so that we may understand what God has freely given us. ¹³This is what we speak, not in words taught us by human wisdom but in words taught by the Spirit, explaining spiritual realities with Spirit-taught words. ¹⁴The person without the Spirit does not accept the things that come from the Spirit of God but considers them foolishness, and cannot understand them because they are discerned only through the Spirit" (I Corinthians 2:12-14 NIV).

"But you have received the Holy Spirit, and he lives within you, so you don't need anyone to teach you what is true. For the Spirit teaches you everything you need to know, and what he teaches is true—it is not a lie. So, just as he has taught you, remain in fellowship with Christ" (I John 2:27 NLT).

The Choice is Yours

Finally, we come to the most powerful gift that God has given to mankind: free will. We can make the choices for our future, or we can allow other people and circumstances to make them for us. Either way, the onus is on us! We can give up, or we can choose to advance; to limit our options or to become a life-long learner; to have an empty life, or choose a fruitful one; to cower in fear or to trust God and be motivated by faith! Our life is a journey that God saw before the beginning of Time. He knows every twist and turn ahead of us. *"Trust in the LORD with all your heart and do not lean on your own understanding. ⁶In all your ways acknowledge*

Him, and He will make your paths straight" (Proverbs 3:5-6 NLT). I chose this for my Life Verse many years ago because I have full confidence that His ways are much more dependable than my own. I can relax with God at the helm.

"Indeed, if you call out for insight and cry aloud for understanding, ^{4}and if you look for it as for silver and search for it as for hidden treasure, ^{5}then you will understand the fear of the Lord and find the knowledge of God. ^{6}For the Lord gives wisdom; from his mouth come knowledge and understanding. ^{7}He holds success in store for the upright, he is a shield to those whose walk is blameless, ^{8}for he guards the course of the just and protects the way of his faithful ones. ^{9}Then you will understand what is right and just and fair— every good path. ^{10}For wisdom will enter your heart, and knowledge will be pleasant to your soul. ^{11}Discretion will protect you, and understanding will guard you" (Proverbs 2:3-11 NIV).

Couch Potato or Conqueror

Progress is not an effortless prize. In the same way that sloth and apathy will get you nowhere fast, being a "spiritual couch potato" will prevent you from becoming "the best ME that I can be". Winning this trophy will require some personal discipline. Decide now that Diligence is a friend that beautifies your life, and not a foe that drags you down. Develop a strong mindset that relishes each challenge to improve and advance. Soon you will find that spiritual exercise strengthens your mind and your spirit just like physical exercise strengthens your heart, reduces stress, boosts your immune system and empowers self-esteem. Every day that you are alive, you have another chance to make good choices; a new opportunity to choose fitness over failure. *"In view of all this, make every effort to respond to God's promises. Supplement your faith with a generous provision of moral excellence, and moral excellence with knowledge, ^{6}and knowledge with self-control, and self-control with patient endurance, and patient endurance with godliness, ^{7}and godliness with brotherly affection, and brotherly affection with love for everyone. ^{8}The more you grow like this, the more productive* *and useful you will be in your knowledge of our Lord Jesus Christ. ⁹But those who fail to develop in this way are shortsighted or blind, forgetting that they have been cleansed from their old sins"* (2 Peter 1:5-9 NLT).

Spiritual diligence will produce a purposeful life. What does diligence produce in our natural lifestyle? Healthy bodies, strong minds, clean clothes, comfortable homes, educational accomplishments, good-paying jobs, happy marriages and fulfilling relationships; well-rounded families and circles of life-long friends are all fruits of a thoughtful life that is lived on purpose. In the following passages you will see some action words that will help you to live your spiritual life on purpose, too:

"Therefore I, a prisoner for serving the Lord, beg you to lead a life worthy of your calling, for you have been called by God" (Ephesians 4:1 NLT).

"I don't mean to say that I have already achieved these things or that I have already reached perfection. But I press on to possess that perfection for which Christ Jesus first possessed me. ¹³No, dear brothers and sisters, I have not achieved it, but I focus on this one thing: Forgetting the past and looking forward to what lies ahead, ¹⁴I press on to reach the end of the race and receive the heavenly prize for which God, through Christ Jesus, is calling us" (Philippians 3:12-14 NLT).

"So, dear brothers and sisters, work hard to prove that you really are among those God has called and chosen. Do these things, and you will never fall away" (2 Peter 1:10 NLT).

"So we have not stopped praying for you since we first heard about you. We ask God to give you complete knowledge of his will and to give you spiritual wisdom and understanding. ¹⁰Then the way you live will always honor and please the Lord, and your lives will produce every kind of good fruit. All the while, you will grow as you learn to know God better and better" (Colossians 1:9-10 NLT).

Rebecca Bryan-Howell

Faithful Stewards are Rewarded

When my children were growing up, I delighted in rewarding them for their childish successes. Whether it was putting away toys or potty-training, getting along with each other or getting good grades at school, I found that incentives went a long way toward encouragement to do their best and to accomplish their goals. God is a loving Father and He not only loves to see His children do well but He loves to reward them for their obedience and commend them for their diligence. He is not a harsh task-master that cracks the whip over us, but a kind and gentle shepherd that leads us to good pastures with great satisfaction and then shares our joy as we are refreshed by them. He delights in helping us to thrive and grow in the life He has given us.

Someday soon, Christ will return to gather all of His own into His fold for eternity. There are great benefits here on earth to pursuing the Christian life to its fullest; but there is also eternal reward. There is a story in the Bible about responsible stewardship that I want you to think about as we close this segment. Remember, the choice is yours to reap great rewards; but there are two sides to the Coin of Life; reward is one, and the other is consequences.

"Again, the Kingdom of Heaven can be illustrated by the story of a man going on a long trip. He called together his servants and entrusted his money to them while he was gone. [15]He gave five bags of silver to one, two bags of silver to another and one bag of silver to the last—dividing it in proportion to their abilities. He then left on his trip. [16]The servant who received the five bags of silver began to invest the money and earned five more. [17]The servant with two bags of silver also went to work and earned two more. [18]But the servant who received the one bag of silver dug a hole in the ground and hid the master's money. [19]After a long time their master returned from his trip and called them to give an account of how they had used his money. [20]The servant to whom he had entrusted the five bags of silver came forward with five more and said, 'Master, you gave me five bags of silver to invest, and I have

earned five more. ²¹The master was full of praise. 'Well done, my good and faithful servant. You have been faithful in handling this small amount, so now I will give you many more responsibilities. Let's celebrate together!' ²²The servant who had received the two bags of silver came forward and said, 'Master, you gave me two bags of silver to invest, and I have earned two more.' ²³The master said, 'Well done, my good and faithful servant. You have been faithful in handling this small amount, so now I will give you many more responsibilities. Let's celebrate together!' ²⁴Then the servant with the one bag of silver came and said, 'Master, I knew you were a harsh man, harvesting crops you didn't plant and gathering crops you didn't cultivate. ²⁵I was afraid I would lose your money, so I hid it in the earth. Look, here is your money back.' ²⁶But the master replied, 'You wicked and lazy servant! If you knew I harvested crops I didn't plant and gathered crops I didn't cultivate, ²⁷why didn't you deposit my money in the bank? At least I could have gotten some interest on it.' ²⁸Then he ordered, 'Take the money from this servant, and give it to the one with the ten bags of silver. ²⁹To those who use well what they are given, even more will be given, and they will have an abundance. But from those who do nothing, even what little they have will be taken away"
(Matthew 25:14-29 NLT).

You have been given talents to invest in this life for God's glory. These gifts, strengths, abilities, and opportunities together form a personal stewardship that He has entrusted you with until He returns. You can choose to be limited by fear, or you can choose the maximum benefits of faith. The sooner you learn to trust Him, the happier you will be because His requirements come with ample assistance from His own hand. Nothing that He gives you to do will be impossible for you. Everything that He places on your pathway will be possible in your capacity, enhanced by His grace. God is good; His plans for you are good; and you can complete your journey with joy.

Chapter Four Summary

We already knew that life was an education; but in this we learned that the world's philosophy of learning is not the one that God wants His daughters to follow. We realized that knowledge is good only as far as it is infused with the wisdom of God, because the wisdom of man is foolishness to Him. As Daughters of the King who are citizens of a heavenly kingdom, we must walk this earth with our eternal purpose in mind. We found out that charm school is a far cry from spiritual etiquette, and that only the School of the Spirit will provide everything we need for living successfully. We learned that our work experience will not only happen in the world around us, but in the church – the Body of Christ, our Christian brothers and sisters – and that our skills will be perfected through our Continuing Education in our relationship with Christ. We can choose to learn life God's way, or we can reap the consequences of being a "spiritual couch potato". Either way, we were reminded that the Master will return someday soon to claim His own, and that He will be looking to see how we have handled the rich, personal stewardships that He has given each of us to invest in this life.

Theme Verse

Proverbs 3:5-6 (NLT): *"Trust in the LORD with all your heart and do not lean on your own understanding. ^{6}In all your ways acknowledge Him, and He will make your paths straight."*

Take-away Gems

- ♦ The wisdom of man is flawed, and can never lead me to God.
- ♦ My education is not limited to what the world has to offer.
- ♦ I have the most trustworthy mentor in the universe!
- ♦ I am free to learn at my own pace, and there is no pressure to perform.
- ♦ God's assignments will always bring out the best in me.

...rn to Privilege

- My "spiritual degree program" is clear, and is customized for my success.
- My relationship with Christ is my Continuing Education.
- I will never lack purpose or fulfillment in the School of the Spirit.
- Diligence is my friend, and her company beautifies my life.
- My talents are my personal stewardship until the Lord returns.

Own It!

Personalize: How can you ensure that your education, from whatever sources, is in agreement with who you are becoming as a Daughter of God?

Ponder: Write down your take-away gems for Chapter Four in your journal or notebook. Choose your nugget: which one is most significant for you right now, and why? List any college or university programs, classes or other educational pursuits you are now involved in. During your quiet time ask the Holy Spirit to help you see these areas of influence from His perspective. Ask Him to direct your steps in using your current or future education for His glory so that you can be purposeful in fulfilling your personal stewardship from Him.

Pursue: Review the Bible verses listed under the subtitle, "Couch Potato or Conqueror". Circle all the action words and do a quick self-check to rate your progress in these areas of personal development. (No competition…this is between you and God!) Accept the challenge!

Persist: Write out the theme verse for Chapter Four on a 3 x 5 card in the Bible version of your choice. Post it wherever you can see it often! Remember that hiding these verses in your heart and reviewing them in your mind will help you to learn to think like God does. Bringing your thoughts in line with the mind of Christ will enable you to become all that you were created to be!

Rebecca Bryan-Howell

Partner: In your Circle of Wagons, share something you believe God has given you as part of your personal stewardship. If you are struggling to invest one of your talents or abilities, ask your sisters to pray with you about it. Encourage each other to act with faith instead of fear in practicing responsible stewardship and living your lives "on purpose" with strong choices.

Chapter 5: Loyalty: The Vine and the Branches

Chapter Four was an eye-opener, because we discovered that the commonly accepted educational systems of our world are missing a vital element! The very element, in fact, that is the most imperative for our success; the only link that can balance every other element for optimal value – the God link! We already knew that the society we live in puts great stock in education at all levels of learning, from early childhood through primary, secondary, and finally tertiary education in universities and/or trade schools. Voices worldwide, speaking out for and about quality education, use a plethora of good words to define it: personal advancement, life-skills, achievement, security and well-being, gift potential, knowledge expansion, community influence, empowerment, professional career path, creative development, economic productivity, sustainable livelihood. All of these are good terms but the qualifying factor is how any or all of them line up to God's values; because without the infusion of God's wisdom, human knowledge is a dead-end! We discussed how education and preparation are necessary but cannot be complete without a biblical foundation to keep us pointed in the right direction. As daughters of the Kingdom of Light – one of only two eternal destinations – we are a part of something much bigger than this amazing earth we've been temporarily planted in. What is our connection to this greatness, and how should it be navigated?

Born to Privilege

Time Lapse Rewind

Nearing the half-way point of our study, it is a good time for a "Selah", which is a Hebrew word for interlude. Selah is a technical musical term showing a pause for accentuation. It is a break, or recess for respite, to draw attention to something of prominence. So, let's stop and breathe for a moment while we highlight some important points that have landed us where we are just now.

We are redeemed; daughters of God who share His inheritance because of our trust in Christ. Our position comes with both privilege and responsibility. We wear a crown of beauty that is driven by our heart attitude, and we travel a road through life with two gifts for success: God to guide us and friends to walk beside us.

We have been chosen by God to engage in His sovereign plans for this earth. He, the Master Potter, takes our lives of clay and continually forms and refines us into vessels of honor through which He may pour His light and truth out to the world. Since our destiny and purpose are in His great hands, we can do anything He wants us to do. He has separated us from the world, in a spiritual sense, and marked us with His seal of ownership to identify us as a special people with a special purpose to carry out as we go through life "in this world, but not of this world".

God's ways are high above the ways of the world, and He desires to groom us in spiritual etiquette, if you will, and to give us free access to an ongoing enrollment in the School of the Spirit where we gain a full and complete education that goes far beyond the things of earth and the limited knowledge of the world. We can choose to excel, and to welcome Diligence as a friend that beautifies our lives as we pursue the fulfillment of our God-ordained purpose and experience everything that He made us to do and to be. We finally understand that the Creator of life and breath, beauty and excellence is also the author of our faith and the designer of a personalized education plan for each of us that will prepare, guide, and enhance our life experiences. How curious that, in the language of education, our "continuing ed" is our literal relationship with Jesus Christ our Lord! How does that work? Let's talk about The Vine.

The Vine is our Life-source

John 15:4 paints a picture of a fruitful vine, such as a grapevine, where branches have been severed from the main stem and can no longer produce fruit as a result. *"Remain in me, and I will remain in you; for a branch cannot produce fruit if it is severed from the vine, and you cannot be fruitful unless you remain in me"* (NLT). The Bible is bursting with passages about this principal truth of the Christian life, that apart from Christ we are nothing. As explained in earlier chapters, when we chose to believe in Christ as our Savior and to give our lives to His purpose, we were infused with the life of God and we became new. We left the old life behind under the blood of Jesus where our sins were forgiven at the Cross. Then we learned that this new place is a privilege to be cherished and guarded; for we also have an enemy, Satan, who will stop at nothing to separate us from God and rob us of our inheritance. This robbery, though a constant threat as described in 1 Peter 5:8, is directly related to our own free will because we are safe in the arms of God unless we open the door to the devil.

I know what you may be thinking, *I don't remember opening any doors to the enemy, and yet look at all the bad things that have happened in my life!* There are many factors here, but the incredible power of free will is that even when other people make bad choices that affect us negatively we can still choose positive outcomes going forward! We don't have to stay in the mud! That's why the Scripture assures us, *"And we know that God causes everything to work together for the good of those who love God and are called according to his purpose for them"* (Romans 8:28 NLT).

If we do not remain in Christ we will wither away; but since we are called to bear fruit for His kingdom we have more hope, help, and protection than the average Jane! We have some very powerful and life-changing options available to us! Jesus says in John 15:5-6 *"Yes, I am the vine; you are the branches. Those who remain in me, and I in them, will produce much fruit. For apart from me you can do nothing. ⁶Anyone who does not remain in me is thrown away like a useless branch and withers. Such branches are gathered into a pile to be burned"* (NLT).

His life in us provides the power to bear fruit, to resist temptation and Satan's traps, and to shine the light of His love to a lost world. The more we follow Jesus and the less we allow our lives to be driven by the influences of the world around us, the more godly fruit we will begin to produce. *"No good tree bears bad fruit, nor does a bad tree bear good fruit. ⁴⁴Each tree is recognized by its own fruit. People do not pick figs from thorn bushes, or grapes from briers. ⁴⁵A good man brings good things out of the good stored up in his heart, and an evil man brings evil things out of the evil stored up in his heart. For the mouth speaks what the heart is full of"* (Luke 6:43-45 NIV). When we truly understand that Christ is the source of our health and fruitfulness we will be dedicated to him and our desire to nourish and protect this relationship with him will grow deep and strong. Like a wanderer in the desert in search of water to survive, we will know that we need more of Jesus to keep our spirit alive and we will feel desperate for him during the segments of our journey that leave our souls parched and dry.

Then the truth will come to bear that it is our ==faithfulness that will most affect our fruitfulness==. The brightness of our character, that "best Me" shining out to this weary world, is defined by the fruit our lives produce; and its source is the life of God that courses through the vine, Christ Jesus, and into the branches, His chosen people saved by grace. *"May you always be filled with the fruit of your salvation – the righteous character produced in your life by Jesus Christ – for this will bring much glory and praise to God"* (Philippians 1:11 NLT).

Rebecca Bryan-Howell

Sprout Up! Growing People Change

In my Bible there is a preface before the book of James which describes its content. One line reads, "This book attacks the notion that becoming a Christian is simply a matter of assenting to a few spiritual truths without experiencing any real change in behavior or thought."[15] In other words, the Christian life is more than "just believing;" it is faith in action. One of the five principal values of the church I currently attend is "Growing people change." Just as a tiny plant sprouts from the ground, sporting only a tiny stem and a couple of smallish leaves, so a new Christian life is tender and pint-sized in its beginning, but far from insignificant! For it has the potential for strength and greatness in its fragile roots that seek out nutrients from the soil in which it was planted. As the wee sprout gains strength, it grows upward and outward until it reaches its full potential – barring the invasion of insects or setbacks from the storms of life. The analogy of a growing plant to the Christian life is common in Scripture, as God often uses the natural to explain the spiritual. A baby Christian, therefore, can expect to thrive and grow with the proper nourishment just as a seedling benefits by the sun, rain and soil; and with proper growth comes obvious change. In fact, Ephesians 4:11-15 gives us a standard of maturity for which to strive: *"Now these are the gifts Christ gave to the church: the apostles, the prophets, the evangelists, and the pastors and teachers. [12]Their responsibility is to equip God's people to do his work and build up the church, the body of Christ. [13]This will continue until we all come to such unity in our faith and knowledge of God's Son that we will be mature in the Lord, measuring up to the full and complete standard of Christ. [14]Then we will no longer be immature like children. We won't be tossed and blown about by every wind of new teaching. We will not be influenced when people try to trick us with lies so clever they sound like the truth. [15]Instead, we will speak the truth in love, growing in every way more and more like Christ, who is the head of his body, the church"* (NLT).

---

[15] "James," in the Holy Bible, New Living Translation, (Tyndale House Publishers, Inc., 2013)

Born to Privilege

Christ himself is our example of what Christian (Christ-like) maturity looks like. Spiritual adulthood is God's plan for us! In 1 Corinthians 13, the apostle Paul states that when he was a child he spoke, acted and thought like a child does; but when he became a man his childish ways were behind him because he had grown in stature and understanding. Again, in Hebrews 5:13 he tells us that as long as we are living on "spiritual milk" we are still babies, and not experienced in the Word of God as a mature Christian should be. Truth to tell, if we are abiding in the vine as explained above, we cannot help but grow and mature as we learn more and more about God and His Word; but this is a choice we make. If we allow the influence of the world to distract us it's like a pest chewing at the connection between a branch and its vine. Becoming severed from our source of spiritual life can happen relatively quickly if we are not paying attention and choosing to be purposefully engaged in "growing up". We've all heard, or said ourselves, "It's time for him/her to grow up!" The reason this is such a common expression is because it is disgusting to see an adult acting like a child! Barring a developmental condition that prevents full maturity, it is universally understood that children grow into adults. As they enter adulthood they will look, walk, talk and think much differently; and their own choices will be driving these changes. They can do it, but sometimes they need a nudge in the right direction. The desire to become all that God ordained for you to be is something that comes from Him; and you can ask Him to work that desire deep into your heart. It is both natural and expected that people will mature spiritually as well as physically.

Pruning Hurts so Good

Another very important aspect of proper growth is pruning! Any shrub or tree specialist will tell you that lack of pruning will weaken the plant and even foster disease. As we grow up in God, walking through this dusty ol' world, we can get a bit shaggy and in-grown. Sometimes our sloppy spiritual hygiene can keep the sun out so long that pests find places to hide and become quite comfortable chewing away at our protective bark! We can get a few limbs growing sideways toward the center – the big 'I' – instead of reaching for the 'Son' where they will be better nourished. As things become crossways in our core, all kinds of problems can result. This is why God, in His mercy, allows things to happen in our lives that prune out some of these rogue limbs that are doing their own thing, against His nature. *"I am the true grapevine, and my Father is the gardener. ²He cuts off every branch of mine that doesn't produce fruit, and he prunes the branches that do bear fruit so they will produce even more."* (John 15:1-2 NLT). Our dedicated gardener will do what it takes to get us growing in the right direction again so that our lives can remain productive and healthy. It hurts, too; and we will feel the pain of the removal, but it will be worth the discomfort to stay healthy, happy and progressive. Hebrews 12:11 reminds us that, *"No discipline is enjoyable while it is happening – it's painful! But afterward there will be a peaceful harvest of right living for those who are trained in this way"* (NLT).

Branches: Parts of the Same

One of the most important concepts that we learn in life – which we addressed in the beginning of our study – is that people need people, and God designed life in this way! I have heard parents say of their children, "How can my greatest joy and most cherished gift also be the greatest source of my pain?" Aside from natural personality traits that cause some people to be more reserved than others, we must accept that we are all in this life together for a reason! God could have ordained human beings to reside on planets of their own with no one to talk to except Him! Instead, however, He created us to live together, relate, and re-populate for a reason. Relationships are important, and they teach us things that we cannot learn on our own. Psalm 68:6 tells us that God places the solitary in families; and any of us who have lived or worked elbow to elbow with other people understands that we naturally rub off each other's rough edges as we cohabit. Proverbs 27:17 encourages us that *"As iron sharpens iron, so a friend sharpens a friend"* (NLT). One of our previous Takeaway Gems was, "God's

Born to Privilege

assignments will always bring out the best in me." Just as parents know best what their children need, so our heavenly Father knows what we need to become everything that He ordained and gifted us to be – our full potential.

The Bible uses a variety of examples to describe the importance of the relational beings that He created us to be. We are branches attached to the same vine, and members of the same body of believers with Christ as the head of the church, as described in Colossians 1:18-20 and Ephesians 1:21-23. Not only do we belong together, but we need one another because we all have a unique contribution that is vital to the whole. Romans 12:4-5 explains: *"For just as each of us has one body with many members, and these members do not all have the same function, ^{5}so in Christ we, though many, form one body, and each member belongs to all the others"* (NIV). A more detailed description – and one worth reading as part of this study – can be found in 1 Corinthians 12:14-26. This passage shows how God has carefully placed all the parts of the human body exactly where He wanted them to be; and in the same way He has placed each of us in His Body, the Church, where we can function best in relation to the other members. Together, with all our individual strengths and abilities, we make up the whole and become complete. Each member will protect and nourish the others in a healthy body because each function is valued equally. It goes without saying, then, that a church body whose members are toxic to one another and tearing each other apart is seriously diseased – which medical science calls "auto-immune disease" in reference to the human body. This is a condition where our immune system mistakes parts of our body as alien or enemies, and attacks these healthy cells (all because of a misunderstanding!)

In every body of believers, just like the physical body, caring for every member brings health and strength to the whole body. Just as the brain cannot tell the heart that it is not important, so must we honor and value each member in the Body of Christ and learn to live in harmony. *"Don't just pretend to love others. Really love them. Hate what is wrong. Hold tightly to what is good. ^{10}Love each* *other with genuine affection, and take delight in honoring each other. ¹¹Never be lazy, but work hard and serve the Lord enthusiastically. ¹²Rejoice in our confident hope. Be patient in trouble, and keep on praying. ¹³When God's people are in need, be ready to help them. Always be eager to practice hospitality. ¹⁴Bless those who persecute you. Don't curse them; pray that God will bless them. ¹⁵Be happy with those who are happy, and weep with those who weep. ¹⁶Live in harmony with each other. Don't be too proud to enjoy the company of ordinary people. And don't think you know it all! ¹⁷Never pay back evil with more evil. Do things in such a way that everyone can see you are honorable. ¹⁸Do all that you can to live in peace with everyone"* (Romans 12:9-18 NLT). This is the only way that we will truly be able to blend together for the glory of God. *"He makes the whole body fit together perfectly. As each part does its own special work, it helps the other parts grow, so that the whole body is healthy and growing and full of love"* (Ephesians 4:16 NLT).

When we are willing to accept that every member is equally important to God and His ultimate purpose, it helps us set aside our titles, petty opinions and domineering attitudes to make room for others and blend with what God is doing instead of being a maverick who wants to be his/her own authority. In this light, it is unacceptable to be too much of a "free spirit"! Don't worry if this is difficult for you; just remember that if you are intent on pleasing God with your life, you can do anything that He wants you to do by His grace and strength. When you are weak, He will be strong and help you to do the right thing. This is another Selah for you: pause and reflect on the fact that the God of the universe is willing to be the Lord of your tiny, brief life! Compared to eternity, our existence on this temporary planet is merely a dot, and yet God is interested in every detail of helping you to become the very best that you can be. He wants you to succeed, and to have the full life He intended. So you can trust Him in all these relational challenges that you may find along the way!

Born to Privilege

Sharing and harmony are God's ideas, as we see in Philippians 2:1-5: *"Therefore if you have any encouragement from being united with Christ, if any comfort from his love, if any common sharing in the Spirit, if any tenderness and compassion, ²then make my joy complete by being like-minded, having the same love, being one in spirit and of one mind. ³Do nothing out of selfish ambition or vain conceit. Rather, in humility value others above yourselves, ⁴not looking to your own interests but each of you to the interests of the others. ⁵In your relationships with one another, have the same mindset as Christ Jesus"* (NIV). His desire is for His children to work together. He wants our spiritual relationships with our brothers and sisters in the Body of Christ to be fulfilling and reciprocal. It is true that we cannot choose the attitudes and behavior of others, and that in working toward healthy relationships in the church (or anywhere, for that matter!) we may often give more than we receive. In the long run, however, our joy will be full and complete by doing things God's way, and by putting others and their comfort above our own.

Remember that there is no "divided loyalty" in God's family. Your love for Him is directly connected to the members of His Body. In fact, our love and comradery for each other is an important part of our authentication and identity in claiming to be His! *"A new commandment I give you: Love one another. As I have loved you, so also you must love one another. ³⁵By this all men will know that you are my disciples, if you love one another"* (John 13:34-35 Berean Study Bible). And God takes this part of our commitment quite seriously. *"If someone says, 'I love God,' but hates a Christian brother or sister, that person is a liar; for if we don't love people we can see, how can we love God, whom we cannot see? ²¹And he has given us this command: Those who love God must also love their Christian brothers and sisters"* (1 John 4:20-21 NLT). Our loyalty to them, and theirs to us, is concurrent with each individual's devotion to God himself. If you have struggled with relationships in the past this would be a good time to remember that powerful Take-away Gem from Chapter Four that says, "God's assignments will always bring out the best in me", as well as a new one for this chapter, "I can choose to allow Jesus to love others through me"!

Strength and Safety: Pulling Together

Just as we see value and success in helping our children to learn how to get along with their siblings, schoolmates, neighbors, and eventually co-workers, God has great purpose in harmonious relationships among His people. We don't have to think very long before we are able to come up with good reasons to work together. First of all, there is support and safety in numbers. Look at Ecclesiastes 4:12: *"A person standing alone can be attacked and defeated, but two can stand back-to-back and conquer. Three are even better, for a triple-braided cord is not easily broken"* (NLT). Not only that, but when we all pool our talents we have more to work with, i.e. Circle of Wagons! We can actually have better judgement when we are listening to a few voices besides our own – especially when we are careful to ensure that the most prominent voice is that of the Holy Spirit, our faithful guide. *"Plans go wrong for lack of advice; many advisers bring success. [23]Everyone enjoys a fitting reply; it is wonderful to say the right thing at the right time!"* (Proverbs 15:22-23 NLT). I bet I know what some of you are thinking about—all those times you tried to work with a committee and you ended up shouting, "Too many cooks spoil the broth! I'll just do it myself." No worries; because this is where prayer comes in. Rather than succumbing to "the little red hen syndrome" let's encourage each other to practice casting all our cares on the only one who can bring it all together! The Holy Spirit is our balancing factor when we are working together to accomplish the work of the kingdom. God's way is not only right; it is the most efficient and the most fulfilling! So, give Him a chance to prove himself in your relationships through teamwork and He will help you find ways to work everything out, and to the benefit of everyone involved!

Some of you may remember a childhood song that was taught in schools and playgroups for decades regarding this vital concept of

Born to Privilege

working together to meet important goals. It was called, "When We All Pull Together", and the lyrics basically explained that it makes us happy to work together because "your work is my work; and our work is God's work"! Matthew 18:19-20 agrees: *"I also tell you this: If two of you agree here on earth concerning anything you ask, my Father in heaven will do it for you. [20]For where two or three gather together as my followers, I am there among them"* (NLT). Again we see in I Corinthians 3:8-9 that each doing his/her part accomplishes the task at hand: *"The one who plants and the one who waters work together with the same purpose. And both will be rewarded for their own hard work. [9]For we are both God's workers. And you are God's field. You are God's building"* (NLT).

If you're feeling some negative emotion about this we should look at a few other factors. First of all, most people who prefer to be alone, or work alone, are affected by at least some level of fear, likely from past negative relationships. Whether you don't trust people or you just don't want the bother of including them in your life, it is imperative for your success to realize that God is not the author of reclusive attitudes. They don't work with His plans any better than a hand that prefers to shake itself free from the arm and the rest of the body so it can flop around independently with no attachment or restriction.

Next, let's consider the problem of "control"; ugh – that's a big word with a lot of negative connotation, and for good reason. Are we willing to recognize that this may be an issue? Have you been told that you're a control-freak? Or have you noticed that you aren't happy unless you get to "have it your way"? How do you feel inside when you're trying to convince someone of your logical perspective and they aren't buying it? Do you burn a little bit when people disagree with you? Or is it comfortable for you to accept and honor the opinions and perspectives of others on issues that you care about? Maybe you've hidden it because you're embarrassed about your need to dominate. Perhaps you have laughed about it in order to minimize its abrasiveness and make it acceptable; or possibly even justified your controlling behavior by attempting to prove it as necessary. Be honest with yourself because, in the Kingdom of Light, no one person should "be in control" of a healthy body of believers. That would be taking the place of God, for He alone is the head of the Body. Capture your thoughts and feelings about this to determine whether a strong desire for control may be one reason you shy away from groups, or retreat to the background when cooperation is requested. The spirit of control is a whole different subject: wide and deep! Suffice it to say, for this chapter at least, that you were never meant to take control of everything in your life – and certainly not other people. God created you to remain under His control – a branch on the Vine of Christ – and to relinquish your desire to dominate so that you can willingly accept His ultimate authority and work together with others who are equally important to Him. This brings balance and harmony, love and respect: an atmosphere where selfish control is never comfortable. This level of Christian maturity is where we can finally realize that God is trustworthy in the workings of His church; we can know and accept that the Body of Christ is a safe place – not because it is perfect, but because it is *HIS*!

Even the world we live in, with its imperfect knowledge and limited understanding, promotes the concept that there is danger in isolation, and it becomes frightening when we need help, which we need more often than we realize! *"I look for someone to come and help me, but no one gives me a passing thought! No one will help me; no one cares a bit what happens to me"* (Psalm 142:4 NLT). Truly, when someone feels this way they are in the danger zone where depression and destruction loom too close for comfort. If you have been in this dark place, or you know of others who have, you know that the order of the day is to fight and flee! These thoughts are tools of our arch enemy who will swoop into our vulnerable places and take advantage of our weakness to destroy our lives or damage our potential. But if someone who cares about you is there, or close by, you have something to grab hold of and hang onto. There is great value in friendship; not just for fun, but for much needed help and support in the hard times, which are many in the scope of a lifetime. The Scripture is clear: *"Two people are better off than one, for they can help each other succeed. ¹⁰If one person falls, the other can reach out and help. But someone who falls alone is in real trouble"* (Ecclesiastes 4:9-10 NLT). In the Body of Christ we will come to realize that the value of our spiritual relationships goes much deeper than common friendships we may develop with people who do not know the Lord; because Christians share a foundation built on the greatest hope in the universe – eternal life with Christ.

You Got This, Girl!

The concept of the vine and the branches may feel somewhat foreign to you if you are a new Christian, or coming out of a religion that was not based on whole-Bible truth. If you're feeling a bit uneasy about looking at your relationship with Christ as a mandate for connection with others, don't allow this discomfort to set in! Remember two things right now: a) The Lord has already given you everything you need to succeed at doing life His way, and b) your arch enemy, Satan, will always bombard you with doubts about anything that is good for your spiritual health and success! When my husband and I were quite young and had moved our family to the northwest corner of Washington State, we were attending a church filled with enthusiastic people who eagerly attended any classes offered to grow their faith. My husband decided to come clean with his father-in-law, who happened to be the pastor, and tell him of his personal struggle.

"I know these are good things, and that they all come from the Bible," he admitted. "I guess I just don't have what it takes to be a good Christian." He was frustrated that he didn't share the same enthusiasm as others, and wanted to be honest about it.

Dad was kind and understanding. "Don't worry about everything right now, Jim. When something comes up that seems impossible, or difficult to identify with, just give it to God and pray, *'This isn't something I can do right now, Lord; but if you are willing to work it into me, I am willing to cooperate.'* God sees your heart and He will accomplish all His purpose for you in His own time."

This freed my young husband to embrace Bible truths and pursue spiritual growth in bite-sized steps without feeling overwhelmed by the magnitude of it all. He was able to put his questions on the shelf of God's grace to be answered whenever the time was right; and today he is a godly husband, father, grandfather and friend to many people who enjoy his ongoing support, guidance, godly influence and friendship. Remember as you move forward from here that God is not limited to your understanding and ability. He will work miracles in your mind and heart when you submit your will into His loving hands and trust Him with it. Meanwhile, here are some ways that we can begin to accommodate this amazing process of drawing our spiritual life and health from The Vine of Christ.

Begin by adopting a determination to just "let Jesus shine" through you. This conscious decision will allow a lot of good things to happen because you are nurturing a mindset to open up and let Him work. When you are sipping cool lemonade through a straw, the straw doesn't have to do anything but stand still. It is simply a tool by which the refreshment is *drawn from the source into the body.* In the same way, when we are willing conduits, the Holy Spirit within us responds to the nature of Christ and draws nourishment from the Vine for our strength, health and progress.

Then, pursue harmony with the Body of Christ by interacting regularly with other believers in Bible study, prayer, and group activities. Step out of your comfort zone and join a small group or volunteer to serve where you can fill a need. Watch, listen, participate and share as you make yourself available to give and receive in church family settings. You will hit a few bumps and face some challenges, but that's when you get to exercise your "vine privilege" to draw more strength from your unlimited source. You don't need to be caught off guard with the obstacles you find in navigating this territory; the Bible already told us what to expect

Born to Privilege

and what we can do about it. *"Be completely humble and gentle; be patient, bearing with one another in love. ³Make every effort to keep the unity of the Spirit through the bond of peace"* (Ephesians 4:2-3 NIV). We have the ability to keep the peace whenever we want to! It's a choice we make to work agreeably with others. Especially if we are all working toward the same thing and can encourage each other toward the same goals, sympathizing with one another's humanness and forgiving the mistakes of ourselves and others (I Peter 3:8). We can even make it work when another member is uncooperative; yes, sometimes a part of the body may be unable to function properly. When this happens in our own human body what do we do? We find out what's causing the problem, and if there is a sickness, or weakness, that needs to be handled with care for a while that's what we do! We don't react to the ailing member in anger, or demand that it buck up and do its part. We help it back to health however we can until it is functional again.

Why is this process so much easier in the human body than in the spiritual body? Here's why: the human body automatically listens to the head. Our brain directs the functions of our body and says, for example, "The right wrist has been sprained and needs extra, purposeful care and support until it heals." Or, "Clean and disinfect the cut on the left knee. Bandage it and keep it clean so that infection will not set in and affect the rest of the body."

This brings us to the other reason this process is easier in our human body: we see every member as our own! We don't say, "a knee has a bruise" but "*my* knee has a bruise". It isn't a random arm that was broken; it is *my* arm that needs to be put in a cast. When we learn to incorporate the second greatest commandment into our lifestyle, accommodating the needs of the Body of Christ will become much easier. *"Jesus replied, 'You must love the Lord your God with all your heart, all your soul, and all your mind. ³⁸This is the first and greatest commandment. ³⁹A second is equally important: 'Love your neighbor as yourself.' ⁴⁰The entire law and all the demands of the prophets are based on these two commandments"* (Matthew 22:37-40 NLT). That's a powerful mandate, and one we can trust the Good Shepherd to work into us when we can't imagine doing it on our own; because this is the answer to His own prayers. *"I am praying not only for these disciples but also for all who will ever believe in me through their message. ^{21}I pray that they will all be one, just as you and I are one—as you are in me, Father, and I am in you. And may they be in us so that the world will believe you sent me"* (John 17:20-21 NLT). Harmony comes easier when empathy abounds; when we feel the oneness in our company and know that we belong to one another.

Next, remember that the Lord wants to help you fight your battles so, if you will let Him, He will gladly destroy the barriers you may find in the way of harmonious relationships in the Body. 1 Corinthians 1:10 reminds us that unity comes as we submit to the authority of Christ. Paul exhorted believers in the early church, *"I appeal to you, dear brothers and sisters, by the authority of our Lord Jesus Christ, to live in harmony with each other. Let there be no divisions in the church. Rather, be of one mind, united in thought and purpose"* (NLT).

Finally, we can rejoice in the results of learning to value other members and treating them with the same respect and honor that we would like to be treated with ourselves. Psalm 133 not only tells us that it is wonderful and pleasant when God's people can live together in harmony; but also that it brings a special blessing from God. This blessing is not reserved for a select few; it can be chosen by any of us when we pursue harmony and refuse contention among our brothers and sisters in the Lord.

Chapter Five Summary

Today we learned that our strongest and safest place to be is "connected to the Vine". This part was easy because we all want to be safe, secure and, most of all, alive! At the same time, though, we discovered that being safe in the arms of Jesus would also place us smack dab in the middle of a huge (and sometimes noisy and

Born to Privilege

pushy) flock of other valuable souls that He is caring for in the same way! We also found out that our loyalty to our loving Savior is directly related to our connection with the rest of His Body, the Church; and that if we don't learn to love other believers who share our faith and trust in Jesus, then we don't really love Him, either.

We realized that in order to have a fruitful life we need to experience spiritual growth, which requires change. We compared our growing faith to a tiny plant that begins as a sprout and grows into a tree. It became clear that staying connected to the Vine was a choice and that, if we were not careful to limit the influence and distractions of the world, this vital connection could be severed, leaving us with no resources. This is where we found out about pruning, and how vital it is for our spiritual growth and fruitfulness to have the shaggy stuff and the in-grown branches cut out. It was interesting to recognize how so many of the hard places we go through in life are actually allowed by our master gardener to rid our lives of things that have cluttered our core and kept out the light of the "Son". Even when it hurts, we saw that God's hand covers us and uses everything for our good when we allow His loving discipline in our lives.

We saw a detailed picture of what the Body of Christ looks like and what we can do to make sure our part of it is working optimally so that we can be happy and healthy in accomplishing God's ultimate purpose for both our individual and corporate lives. We had to be honest in admitting that life is better together because God ordained it that way, and that our efforts against toxicity in our relationships will bring wholeness and value to our experience. Owning the other members as part of ourselves was a concept we found to be imperative to our success; and we saw that what makes it happen is trusting the Head of the Body, our Lord Jesus, to direct our functions in working and caring for one another. We saw how ugly a controlling spirit really is, and realized that we don't have to live with that shadow on our soul if we are willing to let God break its chains. We each have just as much ability to learn the joy of "pulling together" as anyone else. Ultimately, we found that no branch can live apart from the vine or the other branches; that harmony is a choice to live together peaceably, and that unity among the believers makes the Lord very, very happy!

Theme Verse

Ephesians 4:16 (NLT): *"He makes the whole body fit together perfectly. As each part does its own special work, it helps the other parts grow, so that the whole body is healthy and growing and full of love."*

Take-away Gems

- Christ is my LIFE-source; apart from the Vine I will become nothing.
- My character is defined by the fruit my life produces.
- It is my faithfulness to God that will most affect my fruitfulness.
- The God of the universe is willing to be the Lord of my life.
- God prepared me for a special place among the members of His Body.
- Loyalty to my Christian brothers and sisters is concurrent with my devotion to God.
- I can choose to allow Jesus to love others through me.
- The Body of Christ is a safe place—not because it is *perfect,* but because it is *His*.
- The value of my spiritual relationships goes deeper than common friendship.
- I will invite God's blessing by choosing harmony and refusing contention.

Own It!

Personalize: Picture yourself as a branch connected to Christ, the Vine. Think about the life, strength, and safety that are yours because you belong to Him. You are a part of Him; heiress to His

Born to Privilege

eternal riches! Repeat your King's Daughter Declaration from Chapter One.

Ponder: Write down your take-away gems for Chapter Five in your journal or notebook. Choose your nugget for this chapter, either from your gems list or from elsewhere in the text, and write something about why you chose this concept. Which gem was hardest to identify with this time? Do you know why? If not, during your quiet time ask the Holy Spirit to help you understand where those feelings are coming from, and what to do about them.

Pursue: Picture your place on the Vine. Then picture many other branches being connected to the Vine all around you. Are you as comfortable with this picture as you were with "just you and Jesus" in the "Personalize" section above? Review the scriptures in Chapter Five that speak to these connections. Do any of them reveal something you could change in your mindset and/or behavior to make your connection to the Body of Christ easier? If you see it but don't want to do it, admit that you aren't there yet; God sees your heart and loves you where you are. Consider praying Jim's Prayer (under the subtitle "You Got This, Girl!") if you are willing to let the Lord work this out for you in His own time. Then thank Him, and trust Him with the results! No self-condemnation!

Persist: Write out the theme verse for Chapter Five on a 3 x 5 card in the Bible version of your choice. Post it wherever you can see it often! Remember that hiding these verses in your heart and reviewing them in your mind will help you to learn to think like God does. Bringing your thoughts in line with the mind of Christ will enable you to become all that you were created to be!

Partner: In your Circle of Wagons, encourage each other to step out of your comfort zones! Talk about Take-away Gems or chapter concepts that you are struggling with and share your feelings. Open your mind to hear from your sisters and ask them for their thoughts about it. Then pray together that the Holy Spirit will guide you to solve these issues with small steps of progress. If some of you have

Rebecca Bryan-Howell

grown past a difficult phase in relationships, encourage your sisters by telling them how it came about and how God used it for good.

Chapter 6: Dressed for Battle

Chapter Five was the type of material that might be called "the clincher", "the straw that broke the camel's back", or "the turning point". You social butterflies will have to step back for a moment while we introverts stand uncomfortably in the limelight on the front lines of maturity in Christ; because, for us, acquiescing to a lifestyle of mingling with and accommodating a lot of other people is not our idea of comfort and fulfillment! Yet, the Vine concept and the Body concept are not only God's idea, but His directive and expectation for His people. You can't be a branch on a tree or a member of a body without brushing up against others on a regular basis. How do you know you can handle it? You know because you are not your own; God created you with everything you need for accomplishing His perfect will; you just need to let Him help you wake up this part of your spiritual DNA! Remember our verse in Chapter 4 about the School of the Spirit? *"By his divine power, God has given us everything we need for living a godly life. We have received all of this by coming to know him, the one who called us to himself by means of his marvelous glory and excellence"* (2 Peter 1:3 NLT). So don't panic! Just take hold of the tools God has provided for this step in your spiritual growth, namely: a) God has not given you the spirit of fear (2 Timothy 1:7) and b) you can do all things through Christ. I heard one of my favorite preachers say, "And what does 'all' mean? 'All' means ALL; that's *all* 'all' means!"

Born to Privilege

This is a new mindset that all of God's people need to adopt and practice. The body concept makes it most clear because we all understand that caring for every member of our human body – even our least favorite parts – is the only way we can maintain health and vitality. Sometimes we need to do a little research to understand a particular area of our bodily health more clearly; and when we do we are rewarded with answers, new tools, or better progress. We can learn all the best practices for our part in the Body of Christ as well, and we will be rewarded in even greater ways than pursuing health for our physical body affords! Why? Because body ministry is close to God's heart and He will bless every effort we make as we trust Him to work these vital steps into our spiritual goals and life habits. Memorize our key verse from Chapter 5 if you have not already done so. Having this truth tucked inside your heart will go a long ways to helping you incorporate it into your life! No fear! No furrowed brows! Your heavenly father's got your back and He will hold you close through every step of progress as you lean on His strength to do what He asks of you. Go ahead; make it one of Jim's prayers if you need to! (See Chapter 5) "Lord, this isn't something I can do right now; but if you are willing to work it into me, I am willing to cooperate."

Back to You, Dear

Now that we've planted the "better together" seed, we are going to leave it in the fertile ground of an obedient heart while we look at another important aspect of "becoming the best ME that I can be"! Get your boots on, because we are going to visit Bootcamp! When young men and women are accepted into the Armed Forces that protect our country they are provided with uniforms, training, and weaponry that they will need in order to fulfill their missions. Their initiation is a boot camp, or basic training period of 8-12 weeks which they must complete and graduate from in order to move on to various types of individual technical, or advanced, training for their chosen or assigned military specialty or career field. These diverse training schools prepare the service member – through hands-on training, classroom sessions and field instruction – with all the skills necessary to succeed. All the skills except one: the will to win!

This isn't the draft, where you are inducted without a choice. Enlistment is voluntary; and so is your decision to follow Christ. Enlisting, however, is only the beginning. A time will come, whether in the services of your earthly government or your eternal king, when you must decide if you are really willing to take the oath of commitment and give yourself to a greater cause than your personal agenda. After all, our earthly journey is not for R and R! Rest and recreation, refreshment and relaxation are sprinkled all along our pathway if we choose wisely, but they are not the sole purpose for our existence – contrary to what many loud voices in modern society may claim. Your culture shouts, "It's my life!" We have all heard it and have subtly been influenced by it our entire lives; but what does God say about it? We read in I Corinthians 6:19-20, *"Don't you realize that your body is the temple of the Holy Spirit, who lives in you and was given to you by God? You do not belong to yourself, [20]for God bought you with a high price. So you must honor God with your body"* (NLT).

My husband has stories of teaching young men under his command in the USAF what it really means to be "government property"! One young man was bragging about a body piercing he had that was safely hidden beneath his shirt where, as he gleefully retorted, "no one can do anything about it". Since their job was working on the electrical systems of the aircraft, my husband calmly explained to this uninformed and cocky, but naïve, airman how his boasting was about to change his life.

"The first time you touch a hot wire that secret metal ring is going to conduct a jolt of electricity through your body and blow off your (pierced body part). Then you'll get disciplinary action under Article 15 for intentional damage to government property. Your choice, airman; but you might want to rethink that decision."

Born to Privilege

Similarly, we should make a conscious choice to commit to God's way of doing things, lest the petty fetishes we drag along with us become a conduit to our destruction; a danger to our well-being and a detriment to our destiny. The truth is that without Christ we cannot fulfill our purpose, and we cannot serve Him and ourselves at the same time. A choice must be made, and then followed through. (See Joshua 24:15) So how do we balance this truth with our God-given free will? Understanding the reason that God gave us this freedom will help. Galatians 5:13 clarifies it: *"For you have been called to live in freedom, my brothers and sisters. But don't use your freedom to satisfy your sinful nature. Instead, use your freedom to serve one another in love"* (NLT). The Bible also assures us that loyal followers of God's ways will reap the benefits of belonging to His kingdom. *"But if you look closely into the perfect law that sets people free, and keep on paying attention to it and do not simply listen and then forget it, but put it into practice-- you will be blessed by God in what you do"* (James 1:25 Good News Translation). I hope that, with me and with your other Christian sisters, you can wholeheartedly say, "I am free to live as I choose, and I choose Jesus."

Articles of Preparation

So, what oath do you swear? What is your life declaration and solemn promise as a Daughter of God? If you were being sworn in by a branch of the US Military you would affirm your support and defense of The Constitution of the United States against all enemies, foreign and domestic. You would promise your allegiance to the laws of our land, the President of our country, and swear to obey those leaders appointed over you.[16] These same concepts are important to think through as a Christian, whether new or more experienced; because just as our civil authorities govern human affairs God governs our spiritual affairs. He has a government, a constitution, if you will, and a structure of authority using emissaries, both angelic and human, who are appointed to promote

---

[16] "Be Ready to Raise Your Right Hand," Military.com, 2020, https://www.military.com/join-armed-forces/swearing-in-for-military-service.html

His will on earth. As we gain more understanding of how His kingdom operates, we can also graduate from new converts to seasoned saints who have more responsibility in the ranks of the redeemed. For now, though, let's look at the articles of preparation for our tenure of service here.

God is faithful to provide what we need for every stage of growth and service so first He defines the situation we are in. *"Be alert and of sober mind. Your enemy the devil prowls around like a roaring lion looking for someone to devour"* (1 Peter 5:8 NIV). Yes, an enemy! Believe it or not, many believers in Christ can't bring themselves to accept that He has an arch enemy constantly working to invade His territory and steal from His people! One of the most accurate examples on our earth of the spiritual world is, to our great chagrin, WAR. All through the ages there have been power-mongers who cannot allow other people groups to live in peace; either because they covet the land and resources for their own, or they just can't stand to be outdone. It's the age-old idiom "fight to the finish" at work. The spiritual world is no different except that the struggle comes down to two powers instead of many nations. Our war is between good and evil, God and Satan; so we need to be sure we are on the right side. Proverbs 14:14-16 is clear: *"Backsliders get what they deserve; good people receive their reward. [15]Only simpletons believe everything they're told! The prudent carefully consider their steps. [16]The wise are cautious and avoid danger; fools plunge ahead with reckless confidence"* (NLT). God wants us to know that there is danger out there, what that danger is, where to watch for it and how to confront it so that we may resume progress.

Next He explains our resources so we can see what we have to use against the enemy of our souls. The first protection we have harks back to Chapter 1 and our position in Christ. When we were transferred from the kingdom of darkness to the kingdom of light, we became heirs with Christ and He gave us access to His authority through the power of His name.

Born to Privilege

"He replied, "I saw Satan fall like lightning from heaven. [19]I have given you authority to trample on
snakes and scorpions and to overcome all the power of the enemy; nothing will harm you. [20]However, do not rejoice that the spirits submit to you, but rejoice that your names are written in heaven" (Luke 10:18-20 NIV). He is telling us that one benefit of being His daughter is using His ultimate authority to defeat our spiritual enemies. He also makes it plain in verse three of this chapter that He is sending us out as sheep among wolves and it's not a game or a cake walk. He wants us to understand what we are up against, and why. *"For though we live in the world, we do not wage war as the world does. [4]The weapons we fight with are not the weapons of the world. On the contrary, they have divine power to demolish strongholds"* (2 Corinthians 10:3-4 NIV).

After giving us the lay of the land and a description of our mission, He gives us the armor we will need for protection and explains every piece of it. *"A final word: Be strong in the Lord and in his mighty power. [11]Put on all of God's armor so that you will be able to stand firm against all strategies of the devil. [12]For we are not fighting against flesh-and-blood enemies, but against evil rulers and authorities of the unseen world, against mighty powers in this dark world, and against evil spirits in the heavenly places. [13]Therefore put on every piece of God's armor so you will be able to resist the enemy in the time of evil. Then after the battle you will still be standing firm. [14]Stand your ground, putting on the belt of truth and the body armor of God's righteousness. [15]For shoes, put on the peace that comes from the Good News so that you will be fully prepared. [16]In addition to all of these, hold up the shield of faith to stop the fiery arrows of the devil. [17]Put on salvation as your helmet, and take the sword of the Spirit, which is the Word of God. [18]Pray in the Spirit at all times and on every occasion. Stay alert and be persistent in your prayers for all believers everywhere"* (Ephesians 6:10-18 NLT).

My brother tells a story of his minister friend who was invited to speak at a Christian church in the Bible Belt.[17] When he arrived the pastor greeted him with warm enthusiasm. "Well, brother! What has the Lord put on your heart to preach about?"

The young man answered, "I'm going to talk about spiritual warfare."

The old clergyman bellowed, "Not in *this* church, young man!"

With great surprise the guest speaker rejoined, "Really? Why not spiritual warfare?"

"Because," the older man explained, "We live from victory to victory! Jesus has already done it all. The battle was finished at the cross and there's nothing left for us to do!"

With sincere consternation and a bit of wit, the young guest queried, "Well, if there is nothing for the Christian to fight against in this life, why would the Bible be so explicit about the armor of God? Why wouldn't the apostle Paul have simply said, 'Dress casual'?"

The truth is, when God says to put our armor on, we'd better listen if we don't want to get caught off guard by the snares of our enemy, who is literally watching for careless and naïve Christians who will easily fall prey to his devious schemes. The good news is that anywhere God sends us He has prepared the path ahead, and equipped us for the journey; because He is a loving Father who wants His children to succeed.

Bear in mind that all of these preparations we are discussing are whole Bible studies that would be interesting to pursue for further enrichment. Our purpose in this chapter is merely to give an

---

[17] Matt Rosenberg, "The Bible Belt Extends Throughout the American South," ThoughtCo, Updated January 28, 2020, https://www.thoughtco.com/the-bible-belt-1434529

Born to Privilege

overview of the battle every Christian faces and the tools to get through it as attentive conquerors rather than victims of hapless delusion. Romans 8: 31-39 is a powerful declaration of this victory that is ours: *"What, then, shall we say in response to these things? If God is for us, who can be against us?* [32] *He who did not spare his own Son, but gave him up for us all—how will he not also, along with him, graciously give us all things?* [33]*Who will bring any charge against those whom God has chosen? It is God who justifies.* [34]*Who then is the one who condemns? No one. Christ Jesus who died—more than that, who was raised to life—is at the right hand of God and is also interceding for us.* [35]*Who shall separate us from the love of Christ? Shall trouble or hardship or persecution or famine or nakedness or danger or sword?* [36]*As it is written: 'For your sake we face death all day long; we are considered as sheep to be slaughtered.'* [37] *No, in all these things we are more than conquerors through him who loved us.* [38]*For I am convinced that neither death nor life, neither angels nor demons, neither the present nor the future, nor any powers,* [39]*neither height nor depth, nor anything else in all creation, will be able to separate us from the love of God that is in Christ Jesus our Lord"* (NIV).

The last article of preparation for our discussion today is the understanding of how we need to view this battle in order to stay strong. We need to realize that we depend on God and we are enabled by His strength. We could never, as finite and frail human beings, have what it takes to defeat a powerful spiritual enemy, as verse 36 in the passage above seems to describe; but the battle is the Lord's and God wants us to remember that it is through Him that we are able to win it. When we face our own giants, we must remember David of old. *"David said to the Philistine, "You come against me with sword and spear and javelin, but I come against you in the name of the Lord Almighty, the God of the armies of Israel, whom you have defied.* [46]*This day the Lord will deliver you into my hands, and I'll strike you down and cut off your head. This very day I will give the carcasses of the Philistine army to the birds and the wild animals, and the whole world will know that there is a*

God in Israel. *⁴⁷All those gathered here will know that it is not by sword or spear that the Lord saves; for the battle is the Lord's, and he will give all of you into our hand."*(I Samuel 17:45-47 NIV). In the Old Testament, Joshua reminded the children of Israel of this very thing. *"Each one of you will put to flight a thousand of the enemy, for the LORD your God fights for you, just as he has promised"* (Joshua 23:10 NLT).

In it to Win It

It's a cinch we can't win the battles of Almighty God; so, after learning whose fight it really is, the next principle He teaches us is that the strength to win is also the Lord's. We need only ask Him and He will generously enable us with the portion of supernatural strength that is needed at the moment, for He is our constant and ever-present helper. *"As soon as I pray, you answer me; you encourage me by giving me strength"* (Psalm 138:3 NLT). Second Samuel 22:30 adds, *"In your strength I can crush an army; with my God I can scale any wall"* (NLT).

Do you remember the amazing account of the prophet Elisha in 2 Kings 6:15-17? *"When the servant of the man of God got up and went out early the next morning, an army with horses and chariots had surrounded the city. 'Oh no, my lord! What shall we do?' the servant asked. ¹⁶'Don't be afraid,' the prophet answered. 'Those who are with us are more than those who are with them.' ¹⁷And Elisha prayed, 'Open his eyes, Lord, so that he may see.' Then the Lord opened the servant's eyes, and he looked and saw the hills full of horses and chariots of fire all around Elisha"* (NIV). Verse 16 is one of my favorite quotes whenever I'm feeling a little vulnerable out there! Try it the next time fear or doubt assails you! As a Daughter of the King you can always declare, "Those who are with us are more than those who are with them"!

Remember, too, that the more you know the less you fear. Remember how easy it was to surprise our little ones with a "Boo!" from behind the couch as we played hide and seek with our preschoolers? We could hide almost anywhere and not be found. But when it was their turn to hide, we had to pretend that we didn't see them because their hiding places were so obvious! We can get to a point of spiritual maturity where we understand Satan's devices on a level that keeps us from being taken by surprise. 2 Corinthians 2:11 tells us that Satan cannot take advantage of us when we are aware of his devices. Other versions clarify the concept, saying he cannot outwit or outsmart us because we are familiar with his schemes; he cannot get the better of us when we know about his plans; he cannot exploit us when we understand his intentions. We would be wise to pray for a spiritual attentiveness that helps us to identify the signs of a coming storm so we can meet it and defeat it rather than panic and run!

If the battle is the Lord's and it is His strength that is waged against the enemy, it goes without saying that the victory is His as well. No one wants to hold up a trophy and get the accolades that belong to someone else. Some day we will each have the opportunity to cast our crown at His feet and thank Him for all the victories that we had in Jesus! He assures us, *"I have told you all this so that you may have peace in me. Here on earth you will have many trials and sorrows. But take heart, because I have overcome the world"* (John 16:33 NLT).

Our Savior is the mighty conqueror and there is no spiritual entity that does not quiver in trepidation at the sound of His name. Yet, what a mystery that He shares that triumph with little old us! We can stand tall and confident as we face the battles of this life because we know that we are on the winning side, and that no battle is too hard for the Lord of Heaven's Armies to win. Whatever we do in His name will have a victor's crown at the other end! *"But thanks be to God! He gives us the victory through our Lord Jesus Christ. [58]Therefore, my dear brothers and sisters, stand firm. Let nothing move you. Always give yourselves fully to the work of the Lord, because you know that your labor in the Lord is not in vain"* (1 Corinthians 15:57-58 NIV).

Naturally, since we still live on this earthly, physical plane, we should expect to be dealing with all the human emotions that a conflict would bring to the surface. Nevertheless, if we keep our trust intact and discipline our thoughts to agree with God, we will not be overwhelmed, even in the storm. During a very difficult time in my life, I ran across a quote, author unknown, that I framed for constant reference in my home. It says, "Sometimes the Lord calms the storm. Sometimes He lets the storm rage and calms His child." Either way a Daughter of God must remember that, whether in storm or calm, God holds the keys and His Peace holds her heart.

Ready, or Not?

Well, girls…now that we all know it's a war zone out there let's do two things: 1) talk about some of the enemy's devices and 2) share some of the ways God prepares us to be victorious! One of the greatest weapons Satan has against the church is something we have been unraveling throughout this whole book: apathy. The dictionary describes it as the absence of passion or emotion; or lack of interest and concern for things that others find moving. Some of its synonyms are words such as indifference, boredom, lethargy, and even laziness. As Christians, we can't afford to be lazy or indifferent about the realities of who we really are, why we are really here, and where we are really going. We dare not walk around in a stupor regarding spiritual warfare; because skipping it is not an option. On the contrary, we must take an active interest in anything that God deems important to our maturity and success. *"Look carefully then how you walk, not as unwise but as wise, [16]making the best use of the time, because the days are evil"* (Ephesians 5:15-16 English Standard Version).

One of the first Disney animations I saw on television was the story of The Grasshopper and the Ants, from Aesop's Fables. This valuable lesson about lazy presumption versus diligent preparation made a deep impression on my childish mind. Learning from the ants began with the proverbs of King Solomon of Israel. *"Take a*

Born to Privilege

lesson from the ants, you lazybones. Learn from their ways and become wise! ⁷Though they have no prince or governor or ruler to make them work, ⁸they labor hard all summer, gathering food for the winter. ⁹But you, lazybones, how long will you sleep? When will you wake up? ¹⁰A little extra sleep, a little more slumber, a little folding of the hands to rest—¹¹then poverty will pounce on you like a bandit; scarcity will attack you like an armed robber" (Proverbs 6:6-11 NLT). In other words, when you are unprepared, the enemy will surprise you with a trap where you least expect it!

In more recent history, Benjamin Franklin said, "By failing to prepare, you are preparing to fail." Additionally, author Zig Ziglar's famous quote from his book, See You at the Top, has been used again and again in different ways; but I memorized Bobby Unser's version. This former automobile racer whose family of drivers won the Indy 500 nine times[18] said it this way, "Success is where Preparation and Opportunity meet."[19] We are always getting ready for something; let's make sure it's Success!

Deception is another powerful weapon that Satan uses against the human race. We know from 2 Corinthians 11:14 that he appears as an angel of light to lead us astray. He is the master deceiver and the father of lies who will concoct any type of wild falsehood or exaggeration of some fact to bowl somebody over and turn them from the truth. It has been said that Satan is willing to speak 90% truth if he can poison it with 10% error to muddy the water and dilute the message. There is no limit to the evil depths that he will go to draw people into his universal web of deceit. Living with a keen awareness that the enemy of your soul is never going to put his feet up and relax his efforts is the best way to keep you on our toes about the wiles of the devil. Paul told the Corinthian believers, *"But I am afraid that, as the serpent deceived Eve by his craftiness, your minds will be led astray from the simplicity and purity of devotion to Christ"* (2 Corinthians 11:3 New American Standard).

---

[18] "Bobby Unser," Wikipedia, https://en.wikipedia.org/wiki/Bobby_Unser
[19] "Quotes by Drivers," BrainyQuote, www.brainyquote.com/profession/quotes-by-drivers

Rebecca Bryan-Howell

The Bible is full of warnings to help us navigate our path and avoid pitfalls.

One looming obstacle for the modern day Christian is Satan's simple tool of distraction. History is filled with tragic accounts of people who missed the mark or lost their lives just because they weren't paying close enough attention. Look at all the accidents that have changed lives forever and scarred families with heartbreak only because a driver was inattentive on the road he or she traveled. We are all on a journey, and the choices we make determine our degree of progress. *"Look straight ahead, and fix your eyes on what lies before you. ^{26}Mark out a straight path for your feet; stay on the safe path. ^{27}Don't get sidetracked; keep your feet from following evil"* (Proverbs 4:25-27 NLT). When Satan sees that he can't rob you of salvation, he will get in the way of your progress instead; and distracting you from a straight course is one of his easiest ploys. If that makes you nervous you're on the right track. Take some time to unpack it and think it through. You'll be surprised what you find! What is *your* biggest distraction?

Let's talk about gates. If you read the book of Nehemiah you will find the account of the remnant of Israel trying to rebuild the walls of Jerusalem after returning from a long period of captivity; and you will see how desperate they were to repair the gates of their city. They had to work with one hand while holding a weapon in the other because they had enemies with evil plans to prevent them from succeeding. They were tired, and often hungry. We are in the same boat as we work day by day to build our lives the way God intended, and to patch up the places that the enemy of our souls has broken down. The most important gates are completely in our control; our eye and ear gates. Satan has a million tricks to get us to leave our gates unguarded long enough to allow him in with something to contaminate our hearts and minds. Once we let him in through the things we see and hear it can be a hard consequence to bear, as well as a fierce battle to get him out! Have you ever left the door open too long and allowed a bee or a big, nasty fly into the house? Or worse, have you ever thought; *I'll just be a minute...*as you leave the door ajar? That minute of carelessness is often all it takes! You can become frustrated and totally exasperated before you finally get that insect cornered and eradicated! It's a good mental exercise to set aside some time to think about open gates in your life. These gates are called by many names: activities, habits, associations, relationships, mindsets, and every other area of influence that should be protected in order to keep your life free of enemy infiltration. Be open to the fact that you have a lot of gates to repair. The Bible is clear that we all need help with this. The prophet Jeremiah said it plainly, *"The human heart is the most deceitful of all things, and desperately wicked. Who really knows how bad it is?"* (Jeremiah 17:9 NLT) The sooner we are willing to recognize these weaknesses – and that we are all susceptible to them – the sooner we can begin to rebuild the gates of our lives to live more safely and wisely. Ask the Lord to show you where you are most vulnerable regarding open doors. He will help you find the cracks where all those bugs are getting in so that you can more diligently guard the gates of your life.

God's Strategies for Victory

Just as Satan has strategies against us to make us lose, God has strategies against the devil to help us win! We've already talked about the armor of God in Ephesians 6 and many Christians learn to wear it by verbally "putting it on" every day, or at least periodically. This practice will help you to develop a Princess-Warrior mindset that will go a long way in preparing you for what you will face day to day on your earthly pilgrimage. Remember that apathy is a strategy of the enemy to catch you off guard! Putting on your armor will keep you aware of his devices, which we are exhorted to do by the apostle Paul in 2 Corinthians 2:11, as we discussed earlier in this chapter. However, a constant focus on the battle can also weary us to the point of despair and fatigue, just like listening to the negative news that often dominates the media these days. God has an answer for that!

Rebecca Bryan-Howell

Did you know that the power of positive thinking has been around since the beginning of Time? Thinking about the good things in life is not simply a psychological self-help tool – although it does help! Actually, this was God's idea and that's why it's in the Bible, our instruction manual for a successful life! Take a look at Philippians 4:6-8. I really like the New King James version of this passage: *"Be anxious for nothing, but in everything by prayer and supplication, with thanksgiving, let your requests be made known to God; ⁷and the peace of God, which surpasses all understanding, will guard your hearts and minds through Christ Jesus. ⁸Finally, brethren, whatever things are true, whatever things are noble, whatever things are just, whatever things are pure, whatever things are lovely, whatever things are of good report, if there is any virtue and if there is anything praiseworthy—meditate on these things."*

We live in a world of fear-mongering. I'm sure you've heard that term, but do you know what it really means? A 'monger' is a seller, a dealer, a promoter of something. All through world history there have been tyrants and dictators who keep people in fear of them in order to maintain control of the masses. By this point in our study you should know, beyond a shadow of doubt, that fear is a tool of Satan to accomplish his purposes with the human race and he is the head honcho behind all things fearful! The closer we become with our Savior the more discernment we have about this strategy of the enemy; and we begin to recognize it in all its cunning cloaks and coverings. Here are a few that you may have already discovered to be nothing but Fear dressed up in different clothes: worry, dread, anxiety, panic, and all kinds of phobias.

Even a germ-a-phobe, who may be seen simply as an ultra-clean person, is actually afraid of germs; something that he or she needs to trust God for, not be controlled by. Once we take responsibility to do whatever is in our power to stay safe, the rest is up to God and we need to leave it in His hands and choose Peace! Look at the Scripture in Philippians again. Does it say, "Only be anxious about the big stuff"? No; we are instructed to be anxious for *nothing*!

Born to Privilege

How? The answer is clearly stated; by taking all of our worries to the Lord in prayer. So, what happens when we do that? God fills our hearts and minds with a supernatural peace that surpasses the earthly understanding that tells us we have tons of stuff to be worried about! It's all there in that simple passage where Paul told the Philippians how to live without fear; which brings us back to our original point. Think about the good things! Meditate, focus on, and fill your mind with what is true *and* of good report! The more you refuse to be drawn in by the fear-mongers, the happier and more successful you will be – and the safer and more peaceful you will feel about your life.

Another way that fears can control us is by stealing one of God's most powerful weapons for victorious living: joy and enthusiasm for life. When we are constantly afraid of what's happening in the world, or worried about our physical health, we are not only stripped of the peace God has given us through Christ Jesus, but also denied the joy of living. Being afraid of the dark will deny you the joy of a full, harvest moon and the breath-taking view of a star-studded night sky! Fear of riding a bicycle will ensure that you never experience the delight of flying free with the wind in your hair! Having a fear of germs and sickness will banish you on an island of lonely isolation where friendship and comradery will never reside; and if they do pop in from time to time, they will not last long because you will drive them away and wonder why they left. Remember where God has brought you from, and what He has given you. *"You have turned my mourning into joyful dancing. You have taken away my clothes of mourning and clothed me with joy"* (*Psalm* 30:11 NLT). The joy of the Lord was the strength that Israel needed for rebuilding their walls in Nehemiah 8:10; and it is the strength that you need to be enthusiastic about the life that God has given you. If you ever want to experience the abundant life God promised, you will get serious about banishing fear from your thought-life and you will consciously close the gates that keep letting it into your mind.

Rebecca Bryan-Howell

Own Your Weapons; Hone Your Skills

Yes, weapons; and they're not for sissies! If you were not raised around knives, guns and the concepts of weapons training you may be squirming (or even gasping!) right now. But since we have clearly identified the battle that you are in, think about whether you really want to walk out there with no defensive protection. The word 'weapon' has received a bad rap in this generation because the fear-mongers of society want to make it appear as an unnecessary evil. Think about this in a spiritual context, realizing that if Satan was the only one with the weapons, he would win every battle, hands down. God wants us to be safe and victorious so He has given us the means to attain that status. *"Praise the LORD, who is my rock. He trains my hands for war and gives my fingers skill for battle"* (Psalm 144:1 NLT).

When Nehemiah supervised the re-building of Jerusalem's walls, he instructed the laborers to hold a weapon in one hand while they worked with the other (Nehemiah 4:16-18, 21, 23); they carried their weapons at all times. Be careful not to let your mind go to a place of ease and apathy right now! Rather than say, "Well, I don't really believe that's necessary;" or "That's just not me; I would rather trust God to protect me instead;" or "Spiritual warfare is overwhelming to me right now; I just can't get into that;" we need to face the facts. Have you ever thought about the fact that Israel's Promised Land was full of giants? When Moses first sent out the twelve spies to investigate the land of Canaan, ten of them came back scared to death! They said, "That place is full of giants so big that we look like grasshoppers to them! If we go in there they will squash us for sure!" Did God relent and take them to a different place where there were no giants? Not even close; He told them to be courageous because He would fight for them and they would rout their enemies. Because of ten cowards, a whole generation had to die in the wilderness and miss out on their inheritance; and when Joshua finally led Israel across the Jordan River 40 years later, the giants were still there. This time, however, Israel trusted God and took their land; one battle at a time. If God was going to fight their

Born to Privilege

battles anyway, why didn't He just wipe out the giants to begin with? The answer is found in Judges 3:1-2: *"These are the nations that the LORD left in the land to test those Israelites who had not experienced the wars of Canaan. ²He did this to teach warfare to generations of Israelites who had no experience in battle"* (NLT).

Life's journey includes battles; we cannot avoid them. Any parent knows that it does not help a child to save them from every trial or challenge life brings. We teach them how to meet difficulties themselves so that they can learn courage and good decision-making skills for a successful future. This is God's perspective toward His children as well. He has prepared us for the battles of life if we will listen and obey. In His love and mercy, He will teach us the skills we would rather not learn because He knows we will encounter things we would rather not see, and do not expect. Listen and learn so that you can truly and fully *live* with confidence instead of fear.

Praise is another powerful weapon against Satan and his minions. Our heartfelt praise and worship to Christ, the mighty conqueror of Death and Hell, will frustrate and frighten the enemies of our soul. The Bible is full of examples of this. One of my favorites is found in 2 Chronicles 20: 21-24: *"After consulting the people, the king appointed singers to walk ahead of the army, singing to the LORD and praising him for his holy splendor. This is what they sang: 'Give thanks to the LORD; his faithful love endures forever!' ²²At the very moment they began to sing and give praise, the LORD caused the armies of Ammon, Moab, and Mount Seir to start fighting among themselves. ²³The armies of Moab and Ammon turned against their allies from Mount Seir and killed every one of them. After they had destroyed the army of Seir, they began attacking each other. ²⁴So when the army of Judah arrived at the lookout point in the wilderness, all they saw were dead bodies lying on the ground as far as they could see. Not a single one of the enemy had escaped"* (NLT). I love how the people's praise to God threw the armies of their fierce enemies into such confusion that they started fighting amongst themselves instead of coming after

Israel! I often pray that God will bring total chaos to the forces of darkness in a particular situation so that they will lose their focus on the Church, my family, or whoever I am praying for. God delights in overturning Satan's plans and throwing his legions into chaos. There is a lot of talk about "open carry" these days, and state governments are passing laws for or against citizens' rights to not only own weapons, but to carry them openly on their person. Regardless of your views on the subject, you can know that when Satan and his cohorts see spiritual weapons displayed in your life, they will not pounce on you as quickly as the next victim because it is obvious that you are willing and able to defend yourself! Putting on your spiritual armor, having God's Word in your heart, and having His praise on your lips are all things that diminish Satan's power to trap us or to trip us up as we travel the roads of life.

Technical Training is Already Set Up!

Remember when we talked about the difference between basic training and advanced training in the beginning of this chapter? This life that you already have in front of you is the grounds for all of your training. Your basic training takes place here, and your technical training will follow as you grow in your relationship with Christ. Somewhere along the way, each phase of your training and experience will come into play on the path of life set before you. We can step out to meet it with the confidence of knowing the Creator of Life, the Designer of our Destiny and the Conqueror of all evil has prepared our pack for us with everything we will ever need to succeed. One of the most important jobs in the military is the job of the Parachute Rigger. Military paratroopers, U.S. Forest Service Smokejumpers, or civilian skydivers all depend on the diligence and detail of the person who packs their parachute. Their lives are in his/her hands because one mistake could cause them to fall to their death from thousands of feet in the air. Those who train to jump are also trained to trust their riggers. They can't allow fear to sabotage the opportunity or else their mission will go unfulfilled and their training will be wasted. Among humankind there are far too many who have been sabotaged by that kind of fear.

Born to Privilege

Unfortunately, some of these have made the tragic choice of ending their own lives prematurely; yet they have not escaped pain, as they imagined they could. Throughout eternity they will bear the liability of squandering their destiny. Life is a priceless gift; an unparalleled opportunity. But, like the job of the paratrooper, it requires trust to reach full potential. The optimal life experience will never be attained without a willingness to trust God with the outcome. The misnomer of seeking escape, for whatever reason, is that one does not simply elude temporary pain. Suicide's deception is that its victims are forever deprived of life's riches: the depths of joy, the exhilaration of victory, and the fulfillment of completion that comes with facing one's challenges with faith and welcoming one's opportunities with hope and trust. Take life seriously; protect it, cherish it and make the most of it with God's ample resources.

Seeing life as a gift from God is foundational to success; believing in its purposefulness will fuel the fulfillment of your destiny, and understanding its brevity is plain, old fashioned wisdom. We learn about this in the book of James. *"Look here, you who say, 'Today or tomorrow we are going to a certain town and will stay there a year. We will do business there and make a profit.' ^{14} How do you know what your life will be like tomorrow? Your life is like the morning fog—it's here a little while, then it's gone. ^{15}What you ought to say is, 'If the Lord wants us to, we will live and do this or that'"* (James 4:13-15 NLT). I have entered the stage of my journey where I see that there is more life behind me than there is ahead of me, kind of an odd realization. There is always a place to look back to that makes you wonder where the years have gone, which is the very reason we talk about living life on purpose, and to its fullest. Each one's purpose is individual; but God's will always involves other people whose lives affect ours, our life affects theirs, or we are connected in some way where our paths cross. We make choices daily to open doors, set boundaries, resist temptations, welcome friends, accept invitations, donate time, and pursue activities. Has it ever crossed your mind that through all of these avenues we are giving away small pieces of our lives every day? Since we are talking about the full value and purpose of life this is a good time to ask ourselves, "What purpose do my choices fulfill or support? Are they worth spending my Life on?" Stop and read those two questions aloud several times, and think about your life as a savings account given to you by God. Have you ever received a gift card or some birthday cash and frittered it away on things that weren't very important? It's exciting to have money to spend, but when we don't think about it first it can be gone suddenly, leaving us with remorse and disappointment! If we used our paychecks that way, with no regard for a budget, we would end up with dire consequences. We like to look back and say, "That purchase was worth the money!" So, what about your time? You are "spending your life" on the things that fill up your days and hours. Are they worth the investment? Or will you look back and feel like you frittered it away on things that didn't matter very much? Your life is much more valuable than your money and time, too, can be budgeted; spend it wisely! There are many studies on time management that can help you set priorities for life; and just like money, it takes effort to accomplish it! There was a plaque in the halls of WestPoint Military College that said, "Without discipline, today's appetites devour the seeds of tomorrow's harvest."— Author Unknown. Thankfully, however, and by the grace of our loving God, we will have another 12 hours in our bank account every morning until our days on earth are done – which only God knows. Until then, if you have been spending your life on things that are not worth its great value, take heart by what Annie said in her movie, "Tomorrow is a brand new day with no mistakes in it!" Tomorrow is only a day away, and God's mercies are new every morning! Start fresh, ladies!

Live on the Offense; not on the Defense

Do you know what football and finances, housework and holidays, rest and relationships all have in common? If you don't stay ahead of your game, you could lose big! Yes, all of these important things require us to stay on the offense; because if we start running behind we may never catch up! This principle can be applied to many human endeavors because maintaining an offensive, or aggressive, position is a principle of life itself. We have to keep our hands on the ball and our eyes on the goal! Allowing ourselves to fall into a defensive position where we have lost control and are scrambling to regain ground will weaken our resolve and delay progress; not to mention wear us to a frazzle! Thankfully, we have great assurance from Scripture that we have extra support for anything that is important to God. Christ gives us the upper hand, even when we are weak, according to Philippians 4:13. *"For I can do everything through Christ, who gives me strength"* (NLT); and 2 Corinthians 12:9-10 *"Each time he said, 'My grace is all you need. My power works best in weakness.' So now I am glad to boast about my weaknesses, so that the power of Christ can work through me. [10]That's why I take pleasure in my weaknesses and in the insults, hardships, persecutions, and troubles that I suffer for Christ. For when I am weak, then I am strong."*

Be encouraged to know that when Satan tries to steal the ball (your joy and purpose) – which he will regularly attempt – or fouls you in order to force a "time out" on your health, finances, relationships, or life-focus, God Himself will come to restore your faith and strength. *"Stand firm against him, and be strong in your faith. Remember that your Christian brothers and sisters all over the world are going through the same kind of suffering you are. [10]In his kindness God called you to share in his eternal glory by means of Christ Jesus. So after you have suffered a little while, he will restore, support, and strengthen you, and he will place you on a firm foundation"* (I Peter 5:9-10 NLT).

We've already touched on the fact that nothing worthwhile is really easy, and we can expect pitfalls and obstacles in our pathway. During these hard times, however, watch out for the Big Ds: Discouragement and Defeat. These are your opponent's trick plays. If your enemy can keep you discouraged long enough he can eventually defeat you; and his favorite strategy is to cunningly wrap you in a Poor Me blankie and convince you that you deserve to feel this way!

Rebecca Bryan-Howell

Discouragement isn't something you've earned; it's a slap in the face! It's a demonic, life-sucking lie that says, "Actually, you're nothing and nobody cares. You're a failure and you can't do this," which I will now interpret for you: "None of God's promises are true!" This is what Satan is really saying in your ear. Why are you listening?

Now that the light has come on you can confront those lies with the Truth for the rest of your life; because they mock and defy everything you really are! What's your oath? How do you declare?

"I, (insert your name), am a daughter of the King. I bear His name, I carry His authority, I radiate His nature, and I am heiress to His riches."

Own it, and use your position in Christ to take authority over Satan's schemes! Don't back down; instead, be bold! *"The wicked flee though no one pursues, but the righteous are as bold as a lion"* (Proverbs 28:1 NIV).

As a Princess-Warrior, you not only have the authority of the Name of Jesus to cover your own life, but to help protect others within your sphere of influence. The more skill we gain in triumphing over the difficulties of life, the more others will look to us for help in learning to use these tools of success for their own lives. A good example of this would be a scenario of refusing depression rather than submitting to it. You can practice a spiritual awareness that sees it coming toward you or others that you love. Anyone who struggles with depression knows that being pro-active against its onset is well worth the effort! Depression is a cruel master, and one of Satan's favorite places to put Christians behind bars where they cannot function at full potential. You can learn the signs and take an aggressive posture to keep depression from overtaking you and to protect your Gift of Life from all other destructive thought patterns as well.

Born to Privilege

Chapter Six Summary

Wow...this chapter was long and intense because of its great importance to our success as Daughters of God. So let's re-cap the highlights. First we were informed that, like it or not, the path we trod as earthlings is a battleground and skirmishes are expected. We were faced with the undeniable truth that becoming a Christian is more than having our sins washed away; it's taking an oath of allegiance to the King of our Heart. We were reminded about 1 Corinthians 6 which informs us that, contrary to societal perspectives, when we belong to Christ our lives are not our own to do with as we please. Instead we have become a part of something much bigger than ourselves, and much more exciting!

We learned that we need not fear putting our boots on and donning our spiritual battle gear because our Captain provides all the training and tools that we will need to work through the conflicts we may face and come out victorious. We talked about some of the powerful gear that we've been given, from wisdom and discernment to the full armor of God and the comprehensive map of the territory – God's Word, the Bible. We also felt some of the pressures dissipate when we heard that God considers our battles as His own and that He puts His full strength behind us to help us win.

On the flip-side, though, we were shown how we can be our own worst nightmare, regardless of God's faithful work on our behalf. Discovering that our eyes and ears were only two of the many gates in our lives through which Satan would seek to gain entrance woke us up a bit. The understanding that everyday activities, friendships, and patterns can render us big losers made us think about what we need to do to rebuild the walls around our hearts and minds to better protect our interests, and God's. Along the same lines, we learned that disciplining our thoughts to resist all things destructive could literally de-claw Fear so that it could not rule our thinking.

In short, we gained a lot of good instruction about this gift called Life, and found out that if we are willing to take our place, accept our weapons, and practice our winning strategies against the enemies of our souls, we will inevitably protect our gifts, honor our Giver, and gain many victories all at the same time as Princess-Warriors of the Kingdom of Light!

Theme Verse

2 Corinthians 10:3-4 (NIV): *"For though we live in the world, we do not wage war as the world does. ⁴The weapons we fight with are not the weapons of the world. On the contrary, they have divine power to demolish strongholds."*

Take-away Gems

- I am free to live as I choose, and I choose Jesus.
- Anywhere God sends me, He has prepared the path ahead of me.
- In storm or calm, God holds the keys and His Peace holds my heart.
- "Success is where Preparedness and Opportunity meet."
- I win when I diligently guard the gates of my life.
- I'm a Princess-Warrior in training; I can refuse Fear!
- I will carry my weapon of Praise openly to rout the enemy.
- I am a privileged recipient of God's beautiful gift of Life.
- My life is valuable; I will spend it wisely.
- My God-given skills enable me to protect myself and others.

Own It!

Personalize: Picture yourself with your combat boots on. Can you willingly take an oath of allegiance to the King of Heaven to defend your life and His purpose against Satan's strategies? Do you feel brave or fearful when you think about this? Bravery is born out of obedience. Can you trust God to help you obey His instructions for life?

Born to Privilege

Ponder: Write down your take-away gems for Chapter 6 in your journal or notebook. Choose your nugget for this chapter, either from your gems list or from elsewhere in the text, and write something about why you chose this concept. During your quiet time ask the Holy Spirit to help you identify some obstacles in your Christian journey that Satan is using to distract you. Write them in your journal and ask God to give you solutions for overcoming them. Over time, as the Holy Spirit gives each answer, write it down beside the obstacle that you will overcome by it.

Pursue: Think of a creative way to display the storm quote somewhere in your home. Make a poster, a pillow, framed computer art or fun project of your choosing to help you remember: "Sometimes the Lord calms the storm; sometimes He lets the storm rage, and calms His child."

Persist: Write out the theme verse for Chapter 6 on a 3 x 5 card in the Bible version of your choice. Post it wherever you can see it often! Remember that hiding these verses in your heart and reviewing them in your mind will help you to learn to think like God does. Bringing your thoughts in line with the mind of Christ will enable you to become all that you were created to be! Start practicing the solutions in the "Ponder" section above that the Holy Spirit gave you for overcoming distractions and obstacles on your Christian path.

Partner: In your Circle of Wagons, have a healthy and bold discussion about one or both of these two vital concepts:

Life Gates: What are some of these "gates" of influence that you need to protect? How have the walls of your heart/life been broken down by failing to guard these areas? What can you expect to gain by protecting them?

Fears: Talk about fears that rob you of abundant life. State their nicknames (worry, anxiety, control, consent, etc.) and describe how they drew you into believing they were legitimate. Then encourage each other in ways to overcome them and trust God instead. Remind each other that fear is never born of God and any form of it is your enemy, sent to destroy you.

Chapter 7: If the Crown fits...

Chapter Six was like stepping into a swollen creek with the intention to cross over, only to discover that the water was deeper and swifter than you imagined! Consequently, some of you may have crawled out on the other side feeling washed-up and worn out from the experience! But the point of focus needs to be on your survival, because you made it with breath to spare! Despite your twisted tiara and your muddied attire, you survived orientation and came out with a better knowledge of the map, as well as a great overview of your weapons and training. Furthermore, if you're still reading this you have chosen to accept your mission because you have discovered that "the crown fits" and you need to wear it or lose it! Plus, you will soon realize that any Daughter of God who takes the oath of allegiance that He requires looks just as good in the uniform as she does in her royal robes! Remember who you belong to; you have the blood of a champion in your veins. Your days will not all be the same because there are a lot of responsibilities that come with a crown. The good news is that, whether muddied from battle or robed as royalty you are the same chosen one that has the signature of God all over you. We have learned that the Path of Life is fraught with perils and that chancing upon these difficulties may leave us skinned up and scared. Through it all, however, our assurance remains the same that ultimate victory is already ours through Christ; and nobody but *nobody* can take our crown.

Born to Privilege

Esther, a Girl like Us

It's true…read the story. The Scripture isn't detailed regarding all the events of Esther's past. But we know that her guardian, Mordecai, was in exile in Babylon after being taken captive from Jerusalem by King Nebuchadnezzar; and that the reason he was raising this little girl was because she had no living parents. (Esther 2:6-7) Whether our darling Hadassah, her Jewish name, lost her parents in the conflict that enslaved her people, or had been under Mordecai's care previous to the captivity, she had a hard childhood either way. Some of us can relate to that. She was in a place that was not her home. Pick out a season in your own life when you felt like you didn't belong. She didn't expect to be taken from her safe place to the palace haram for a beauty contest, and she certainly did not expect to win! That part might be a stretch for most of us, but the point is that her destiny was driven by things that she did not choose for herself. I would venture to say that none of us are exempt from this. We all have to admit that hard things happen in our lives due to the choices of others! So, yes; Hadassah was a girl like you.

The meaning of her Hebrew name is curious: myrtle tree. The myrtle is a flowering plant native to the Mediterranean region, which is known for the fragrance of its leaves; but guess what? The fragrance is not released until the leaves are crushed![20] What an amazing fact in regards to Esther's story. Her little life had been crushed more than once before she wore her regal crown. Even then, as the account is written, she feared for her life just as much in her place of prominence and had to be reminded by the voice of her God-ordained history that the purpose for which she wore this crown was greater than herself. We find the wise counsel of Mordecai in Esther 4:14: *"…And who knows but that you have come to your royal position for such a time as this?"* (NIV)

---

[20] "Etymology & Historical Origin of the baby name Hadassah," OhBaby! NAMES, https://ohbabynames.com/all-baby-names/hadassah/

Wherever you came from, whatever events have shaped your destiny until today, you who have received Christ as your Savior and Lord now find yourself standing in a royal court, redeemed and commissioned to take part in kingdom business. To rebel at any stage of that ancient process would have cost Esther her life; but she entrusted her destiny to the God of her fathers and was rewarded for her faithfulness in cooperating with His greater plan and higher purpose. She did not die at the hands of Israel's ancient enemy[21] through Haman, the Agagite. She conquered him with an obedient heart; a heart that bowed to the King of Heaven as second to none. Where does your loyalty lie? Will you, as a Daughter of God Most High, recognize that you were also born for such a time as this? Can you make Him second to none, and trust your destiny into His powerful and protective hands? If so, reach out and take the crown that fits; and step up to take your station.

A Place of Honor

If the crown fits, wear it with integrity, understanding that the place God has lifted you to as His heir is honorable, indeed. We've talked about what it means to take an oath of allegiance to Christ, but are you aware of His commitment to you? *"Anyone who wants to be my disciple must follow me, because my servants must be where I am. And the Father will honor anyone who serves me"* (John 12:26 NLT). In order to learn from Him we must follow Him, and to serve Him we must be where He is. These are choices we must make and disciplines that we must apply yet they need not be weights to burden our journey. When we accept His love for us and believe in His purpose for us, we relax and lean into Him to find that His yoke is easy! Jesus said in Matthew 11:29-30, *"Take my yoke upon you. Let me teach you, because I am humble and gentle at heart, and you will find rest for your souls. ³⁰For my yoke is easy to bear, and the burden I give you is light"* (NLT). Now, instead of seeing everything as a sacrifice, we see the yoke as a

---

[21] Emil G. Hirsch, M. Seligsohn and Solomon Schechter, "Haman the Agagite," Jewish Encyclopedia, 1906 unedited full text, http://www.jewishencyclopedia.com/articles/7124-haman-the-agagite

Born to Privilege

blessing instead of a burden. Remember in Chapter One where we learned that we can choose whether to see our crown as a privilege or an obligation? Faith turns problems into possibilities and the yoke of responsibility becomes a welcome avenue that propels us forward into new territory.

Our service to God is a great honor, the highest and best use of our earthly lives. It is the epitome of fulfillment and security; there is no master who could love us more than Jesus does. *"The LORD says, 'I will rescue those who love me. I will protect those who trust in my name. ^{15}When they call on me, I will answer; I will be with them in trouble. I will rescue and honor them'"* (Psalm 91:14-15 NLT). He honors our decision to trust Him with the most important things in life. He responds to our allegiance with patience and grace, however hesitant we may be; and demonstrates His love to use in a multitude of ways when we look to Him. I talked to a woman once who loved the Lord but felt that her needs remained unmet, though she had prayed for years that God would make changes in her life. I looked at her and asked, "What kind of changes?"

She replied woefully, "A better job…more money. I can barely afford the gas to drive to church and back so I can't be involved in anything."

As I prayed for her later, I saw the inside of a cottage. It was clean and cozy, but very small, with a heavy door that was closed and had no window. She stood with her back to the door, looking around her cottage in despair. Outside the cottage was a far-reaching landscape in all directions full of hills and trees and meadows. From the door of the cottage a wide, clear pathway curled through the land as far as the eye could see. It came to me so clearly that we are each responsible to open our own door and step out. We must look around, listen, move forward, and investigate the land if we are to discover its possibilities. As long as we stay closed up inside our cottage moaning about its inadequacies, we will never experience the opportunity for change and growth that God has planted just outside of our comfort zone. Do something, ladies! Step out, and then allow God to guide you. You may have Jesus at the wheel, but a moving vehicle is much easier to steer than one that is parked against a curb! What is the defining element that brings change in these two scenarios? It is the difference between sitting and searching. The Lord makes it clear: *"Ask and it will be given to you; seek and you will find; knock and the door will be opened to you. [8]For everyone who asks receives; the one who seeks finds; and to the one who knocks, the door will be opened"* (Matthew 7:7-8 NLT). Too many times we ask and beg without seeking or knocking on doors! We can't expect to find anything when we are not looking for it. Accepting our station means acting on our options. So, where do you begin?

A Cut Above

One of the first responsibilities we must learn to carry out as God's daughters is to recognize the vital nature of choosing to live separate from the world around us; not because we are better than anyone but because we belong to a kingdom with a different value system and a different set of objectives. When we talked about this in Chapter Three we learned that God calls us out of this world in a spiritual sense even though we live here in a physical sense. This is about understanding that Satan is the god of this world and that without God it is a place of darkness and ruin. When Jesus walked this earth He was criticized for eating with "publicans and sinners". In the gospels we find that His answer to the snobbish Pharisees was that He did not come to call righteous people, but sinners to repentance. When we talk about being separate, a cut above the rest, it is not to look with disdain at people who don't know Christ. It's about learning to love them as Jesus did while still loving God and honoring Him with every aspect of our lives. It is not to be elevated above this earthly plane, but to enter a plane where we are able to live on the earth and walk in the Spirit at the same time. This is as simple as understanding that we can be in tune with the Holy Spirit, our teacher and guide, while carrying out the duties and activities of life on planet earth. It is living for God without

Born to Privilege

becoming entangled in things that would hold us back from serving the Lord wholeheartedly. *"No one serving as a soldier gets entangled in civilian affairs, but rather tries to please his commanding officer. ⁵Similarly, anyone who competes as an athlete does not receive the victor's crown except by competing according to the rules"* (2 Timothy 2:4-5 NIV). We are called to a higher standard of living life from God's point of view! From this viewpoint we work and learn and grow alongside everyone else – including those who are without Christ and are living by the standards of the world – while shining the light of truth wherever we go.

In order to live on this higher ground, we must learn to be patient with others and with ourselves. Those who live by a worldly standard will cross us and test our resolve. At the same time, we will see things in ourselves that need work and we can lose heart with the process of Christian maturity. The key to this dilemma is waiting on the Lord; and our Bible heroes and heroines explain it perfectly. *"Let all that I am wait quietly before God, for my hope is in him"* (Psalm 62:5 NLT). The Psalmist of Israel knew that the quiet meditations of his heart toward his Maker were the fuel to keep him growing and thriving. The King James Version uses the word 'expectation' here instead of the word 'hope'. We can learn from David that all our expectation must come from the Lord, just as we studied earlier that our source of spiritual vitality is our relationship with Christ. These concepts don't have to be difficult if we take them a day at a time. When we were little girls learning to fix our hair it was a huge challenge just to brush out the tangles! We even left a few in there because it hurt too much. As we practiced and experimented day by day, however, we learned how to curl and braid, cut, twist, and color our hair into a variety of elaborate and creative dos! Everything worthwhile takes time. *"So do not throw away this confident trust in the Lord. Remember the great reward it brings you! ³⁶Patient endurance is what you need now, so that you will continue to do God's will. Then you will receive all that he has promised"* (Hebrews 10:35-36 NLT).

God's ways are perfect, and *perfect* seems a long way off. Just remember that God is at work in you and He will provide everything you need to get where you are going! *"But they that wait upon the LORD shall renew their strength; they shall mount up with wings as eagles; they shall run, and not be weary; and they shall walk, and not faint"* (Isaiah 40:31 KJV). One day you will look back at your journey and wonder why it seemed so hard, just like a professional hairdresser smiles at her memories of bad hair days.

Your quiet time before the Lord will be of priceless value to you as you grow in God. We are learning to do His bidding and we can't accomplish that if we are not present, and listening, when He speaks! Developing your personal prayer-life is another subject, as are each of these steps to growth discussed in this book; but right now setting time aside to talk to God is vital. Cherish your connection to the Vine of Christ and you will grow strong. He will teach you how to make it a priority if you will ask for His help.

Let's Talk Grace

We've all heard grace defined as "undeserved favor". We know that except by the grace of God none of us could be saved because we would all get the death penalty for our sins. God, in His mercy, sent His Son, Jesus, to take the rap for all who believe so that we could be saved from that penalty by the blood of Christ through His death on the cross of Calvary. That's grace; and what God has given us we must extend to others. Grace is your tiara; and offering second chances, forgiveness, compassion, mercy, and love to the unlovable are jewels in that crown. History overflows with tales of wicked and cruel kings, queens, and various rulers who abused their subjects and cheated their way to the top. Our king is kind and good; He wants us to emulate those qualities to the world. Oh, don't worry; He knows we are all learning and He will be generous in dealing with our blunders regarding each other. We need to think of these as growing pains to push through! 2 Peter 3:18 tells us to "grow in grace" so we know that it's a process that we all go through. Paul explains his own experience with it in 2 Corinthians 1:12 *"We can say with confidence and a clear conscience that we have lived with a God-given holiness and sincerity in all our dealings. We have depended on God's grace, not on our own human wisdom. That is how we have conducted ourselves before the world and especially toward you"* (NLT). Just like any other skill, we will learn to conduct ourselves with grace toward our fellow man if we are willing to work at it. These are areas where we can demonstrate the 'cut above the rest'; since our world has so many voices telling us to treat people however they deserve to be treated. We are held to a higher standard because, sinner or saint, we recognize that human beings are created in the image of God and He loves the lowest criminal as much as He loves the rest of us. Learning how to love the world like God does is impossible in our own strength; but here is a challenge you can give back to the Lord with Jim's Prayer from Chapter Five. Ask God to work this out for you in His own time; then thank Him for it and trust Him with the results. We are all works in progress, and the Master Potter knows how best to form the clay.

Maintaining an attitude of gratefulness to God for His patience toward you will help you to have more patience with others. Love covers a multitude of sins, says 1 Peter 4:8; and herein lies a slight dilemma. God is love, yet He is a righteous judge before whom no sin will go unpunished. His righteousness does not tolerate sin; yet His mercy makes provision to save us from its penalty. Our understanding has to be that our sin is not covered because God winks and looks the other way; but only because the blood of Jesus Christ makes atonement for it. Our sins are not swept under a rug or closed up in a closet to be hidden from view. They are gone; we have been cleansed and made new through the righteousness of Christ! We are no longer sinners since we have been redeemed. If we are not careful to keep it straight in our minds that sin is something to be saved from, we can get into the weeds of tolerance and develop a benign attitude toward sinful lifestyles while trying to love the sinner. Accommodating sin for the sake of someone else is the same as harboring a criminal, which is no more condoned by our righteous judge than committing the sin ourselves. Only God will judge the sinner, while it remains our responsibility to show them His love and grace. In our loving, however, we are held accountable to adhere to God's standard by offering the Good News to those who are without Christ.

Ignoring sin is a compromise to the truth and puts us in danger of the consequence expressed in Ezekiel 33:7-9 where God told the prophet that if he failed to warn the people and they died in their sins, that prophet would be held accountable. This is not to be held over our heads as condemnation, because we are neither responsible for the choices of others, nor in a position to judge them for their sins. At the same time, however, an apathetic attitude can easily be taken as acceptance (or dismissal) of their behavior. Our commission, by Christ's example, is to give the gospel to those who need it, knowing that it is the only provision made to save their lives from destruction. We must learn to see the sin for what it is – a wrong choice someone makes that entraps them and brings God's judgement – while focusing on the sinner for who he is – a person made in God's image who stands in desperate need of the freedom Christ has provided for us all. As we learn to extend God's grace to others, He will give us wisdom in how to truly love them while still giving them the truth that will set them free. The goal of love is not to keep people comfortable, but to show them their value in God, and His promise of abundant life in Christ. We want others to find eternal purpose for their lives, just as we have found purpose for our own. *"Don't copy the behavior and customs of this world, but let God transform you into a new person by changing the way you think. Then you will learn to know God's will for you, which is good and pleasing and perfect"* (Romans 12:2 NLT). Christianity is not a religion, but a relationship and a lifestyle. It is not a diet of restrictions, but an ongoing state of happy and healthy living. *"Instead, let the Spirit renew your thoughts and attitudes. [24]Put on your new nature, created to be like God—truly righteous and holy"* (Ephesians 4:23-24 NLT). Living by the Bible is a choice we make, and one that others can see. Loving God means valuing others and caring for their needs, knowing that presenting the love

Born to Privilege

of Christ in this way can draw them to the truth that will save their souls. Mercy and Truth work together.

Don't Forget Deportment

During my lifetime, the church in general morphed from a place where the lost came for salvation to a place where the lonely came for acceptance. Not to get sidetracked on the purpose of the church, I only mention this because, in making the church more acceptable in the eyes of the seeker, too many leaders lowered their own standard of Christian living in the process. Stay with me here, because these concepts are fuel for some lively discussion that would send us off track in a hurry! Here's my point: as Daughters of the King we should conduct ourselves in a way that honors God in all aspects of our lives, which we briefly discussed in the above section, *A Cut Above*. When we talk of royalty, everyone expects that the station comes with a certain type of deportment. A queen's bearing will include manners, postures, attitudes and practices that demonstrate respect for the authority of the crown and dedication to the ideals and principles of the realm they represent. This kind of standard differentiation is often scoffed at by the western world, especially in countries where government by the people allows us to vote our leaders in and out. It can be seen as uppity, superficial, or unnecessarily formal, as well as out of touch with the real world and possibly prone to corruption. Our forefathers came to this land to be free of all that and to form a government that was more about the people and their values than monarchs holding all the power and keeping it in the family by hook or by crook. As a western American girl, I can be as independent as anyone and I cherish that freedom for which so many bled and died. That said, stick with me while I present a balanced medium.

Like it or not, leadership comes at a price. Have you ever heard the phrase, "It's lonely at the top"? That's because there is a lot of space between the ground floor and the Presidential Suite! You can't be both places at once and function properly. You are either the teacher or the student; the parent or the child; the boss or the employee; the leader or the follower and the list goes on. We talked about recognizing our position as a privilege, and the way we live that out is by accepting God's standard of separation from the world and taking our place among other leaders who understand that their actions and attitudes, their words and their ways, are an example of quality and integrity to everyone around them. It's not lonely if you know who you are and why you're here. Once we belong to Christ and begin our Christian journey, we're on an automatic leadership track because from now on our standard of living will be a cut above the rest. The balance is this: we all started out at the same place: a human being who needed Jesus. That's always going to be our common ground with the rest of the world. Yet, we moved up to higher ground when we met the Lord; we were separated from the world and given a mission in His kingdom. This makes us both human and immortal, in the world but not of the world, both physical and spiritual; and that's the perfect balance that we only find in Christ. We will act, walk, and talk like the royalty that God created us to be; not to look down on anyone else, but to be the hand that is able to pull them up when they're down. Our new nature changes everything for the good because God is in us and He loves the world around us. *"The mind governed by the flesh is death, but the mind governed by the Spirit is life and peace"* (Romans 8:6 NIV). Elevating any human leader too high can be detrimental; and humans tend to put those they follow in precarious places with larger-than-life titles. When this type of promotion comes tumbling down it is often warranted, and for the good of all; but spiritual responsibility is different. Toppling from a man-made pedestal is a lot different than jumping from a place of spiritual high ground back into the mud! Our authority is given by Jesus Christ and we are responsible to use it for the purposes He intended.

Keepers of the Trust

There is no doubt that it's hard to live fully and responsibly in this physical world while walking fully and responsibly in the Spirit; but it is part of the package, and something we can all learn to do

Born to Privilege

well! One concept that will help us with this is in Revelation 3:11. *"I am coming soon. Hold on to what you have, so that no one will take your crown"* (NIV). We can change our mindset to a spiritual one that is thinking on eternal values and always anticipating the coming of Christ. This enables us to hold loosely to all the connections we have with life on earth and hold tightly to everything that is coupled with eternity. Let's look at some of the characteristics of an honorable life that motivate us to keep spiritual values at the forefront.

"By his divine power, God has given us everything we need for living a godly life. We have received all of this by coming to know him, the one who called us to himself by means of his marvelous glory and excellence. ⁴And because of his glory and excellence, he has given us great and precious promises. These are the promises that enable you to share his divine nature and escape the world's corruption caused by human desires. ⁵In view of all this, make every effort to respond to God's promises. Supplement your faith with a generous provision of moral excellence, and moral excellence with knowledge, ⁶and knowledge with self-control, and self-control with patient endurance, and patient endurance with godliness, ⁷and godliness with brotherly affection, and brotherly affection with love for everyone. ⁸The more you grow like this, the more productive and useful you will be in your knowledge of our Lord Jesus Christ. ⁹But those who fail to develop in this way are shortsighted or blind, forgetting that they have been cleansed from their old sins. ¹⁰So, dear brothers and sisters, work hard to prove that you really are among those God has called and chosen. Do these things, and you will never fall away. ¹¹Then God will give you a grand entrance into the eternal Kingdom of our Lord and Savior Jesus Christ" (2 Peter 1:3-11 NLT).

We have talked about 2 Peter 1:3 more than once, but the rest of this passage is packed full of goodies. We will use this Scripture in our *Own It* exercises at the end of the chapter, so I will only refer to it briefly here. The passage begins with the key to success in the honorable life: "By His divine power..." Remember that you cannot grow these things on your own; they happen by the power of the Holy Spirit at work in you. Our part is to listen and respond to His process. These are God's promises that enable us to be who He wants us to be in this world, and all of them work together and build upon each other to grow us up in Christ and expand our horizons. Take note, toward the end, the warning of what happens to those who refuse to develop these things in their lives. I use the word 'refuse' instead of 'fail' because you can only fail if you refuse! We are given the great confidence that if we determine to grow as God wants us to, we will never fall away; and we will be ready for the return of Christ when He comes for His own.

In addition to the list in 2 Peter 1:3-11 above, I want to highlight four more characteristics that I believe are imperative for this honorable life that we are pursuing together. The first one is humility. This trait is not popular in our culture because it is considered weak. But the opposite of humility is pride, which God hates. 1 Peter 5:5-6 reminds us that God opposes the proud but gives favor to those who are humble. A prideful attitude will destroy us eventually. *"Pride goes before destruction, a haughty spirit before a fall"* (Proverbs 16:18 NIV). On the other hand, we can forego the disgrace that always results from prideful attitudes and choose wisdom instead. *"Pride leads to disgrace, but with humility comes wisdom"* (Proverbs 11:2 NLT). I don't want to belabor the point because we've talked a lot about keeping our minds in the right place by remembering where all our help and blessing comes from. We will be rewarded for giving God the glory as we succeed in life; and we will succeed when we live the life God ordained for us. *"True humility and fear of the LORD lead to riches, honor, and long life"* (Proverbs 22:4 NLT). But more than that, I want all of you to recognize that this kind of humility – the kind that bows with a grateful and obedient heart before the God of the universe – is the best beauty treatment you could ever find to enhance your person. *"Don't be concerned about the outward beauty of fancy hairstyles, expensive jewelry, or beautiful clothes. ⁴You should clothe yourselves instead with the beauty that comes from within, the **unfading beauty of a gentle and quiet spirit**,*

Born to Privilege

which is so precious to God" (I Peter 3:3-4 NLT). This, interestingly enough, is further evidence that we are all made of the same clay; for the things that make us most beautiful in God's eyes do not come through the gene pool and cannot be purchased by any amount of worldly wealth. When it comes to true beauty we all get there the same way, girls; by submitting to the supernatural work of the Holy Spirit in our lives and allowing His glorious nature to supersede our own. Humility is the beauty treatment that comes on the lips of this simple prayer, "Change me, Lord. I want to be more like you."

Reverence is the next quality I believe every heiress needs in her character clutch; because it should go everywhere with us like a compact mirror in an evening bag. Did you know God told Israel that His covenant was meant to bring them life and peace, but it would require them to show reverence for Him and for His name? We live in such a world of entitlement that we get used to believing that people have a right to just about everything without lifting a finger for it! God's view is the opposite of that. No one is more generous than He and yet He makes it clear that the life and breath He freely gave us was not so we could demand things of Him. Rather, it was given for us to praise and honor Him with; and when we do we are amply rewarded with more than we could ever think to ask for. I've often wondered how this modern world, constantly squawking for more benefits, would be affected if they could hear just 30 seconds of the heavenly hosts praising our Creator. *"All heaven will praise your great wonders, LORD; myriads of angels will praise you for your faithfulness. ⁶For who in all of heaven can compare with the LORD? What mightiest angel is anything like the LORD? ⁷The highest angelic powers stand in awe of God. He is far more awesome than all who surround his throne"* (Psalm 89:5-7 NLT).

A proper reverence for God affects our choices: *"Because we have these promises, dear friends, let us cleanse ourselves from everything that can defile our body or spirit. And let us work toward complete holiness because we fear God"* (2 Corinthians 7:1

NLT). We can "practice His presence" in a way that keeps us aware of His awesome oversight in the affairs of men. He is mighty, and glorious above anything we have ever known! Yet He sent His Son to atone for our sins so that we could spend eternity with Him. How awesome is that! We are busy being people, doing things and going places; sometimes to the point of forgetting what is most important about our little spot called Life. We were created for God's pleasure, and He acknowledges His interest in us every single day as He protects, provides, teaches and guides us. How often do we acknowledge Him? How willingly do we stop and reflect on who He really is in the universe? We can encourage each other to give Him the reverence He requires. The Psalmist penned God's words to us in Psalm 46:10, *"Be still, and know that I am God! I will be honored by every nation. I will be honored throughout the world"* (NLT).

Determination is a word we all understand, and it is the next character quality I want you to develop and cherish. The passage above lists "patient endurance". Let's call that 'patience' and expand endurance into 'determination'. Some are born with determination; I think I was. But you can have it if you want it, and you do! You can get more mileage out of everything by exercising just a little more discipline to follow through. We have all heard the famous line from a speech by Winston Churchill to a class of students at Harrow School in October of 1942, "...never give in, never give in, never, never, never...except to convictions of honor and good sense."[22] This exhortation clearly describes a choice that we all have: to give in, or to persevere. Learn to be determined, ladies, especially about the things that matter most. You are running for more than the finish line, you are running to win!

"Don't you realize that in a race everyone runs, but only one person gets the prize? So run to win! [25]*All athletes are disciplined in their training. They do it to win a prize that will fade away, but we do it for an eternal prize.* [26]*So I run with purpose in every step. I*

---

[22] Winston Churchill, "Never Give In," in 1941-1946 Speeches, National Churchill Museum, https://www.nationalchurchillmuseum.org/never-give-in-never-never-never.html

Born to Privilege

am not just shadowboxing" (I Corinthians 9:24-26 NLT). Discouragement will dog you if you stand still and look bleakly down the road, and you can give in to that if you want to; but if you put your hand to the plow and determine to finish, you will get there eventually. "One step at a time" may sound like a worn out cliché to you today; but keep moving and you will be one step ahead of discouragement all the way, which means you win.

For the finishing touch, let's look at service. Finding a place to serve in your local body of believers is imperative for your progress, your enrichment, and your fulfillment as a Daughter of God. Not to mention, your preparation for the Marriage Supper of the Lamb. Do you realize what prepares the Bride of Christ for His wedding feast? Take a look at Revelation 19:7-8: *"Let us be glad and rejoice, and let us give honor to him; for the time has come for the wedding feast of the Lamb, and his bride has prepared herself. ⁸She has been given the finest of pure white linen to wear. For the fine linen represents the good deeds of God's holy people"* (NLT).

An earthly bride gets herself ready for the ceremony by donning her wedding gown and her costly pearls. The wedding garments of the Bride of Christ, the world-wide church of believers who await His return, will be spun with the golden threads of good deeds. Serving others is a biblical mandate and, as I have repeated often, a whole different study! But suffice it to say that finding places to give your time and talents where they are really needed, and not just where you get money or kudos for your skillset, is very precious to God. Remember the story of the banquet host in the gospels? Jesus wanted to make it clear that service, not prestige or position, was the most important factor. *"Then Jesus said to his host, 'When you give a luncheon or dinner, do not invite your friends, your brothers or sisters, your relatives, or your rich neighbors; if you do, they may invite you back and so you will be repaid. ¹³But when you give a banquet, invite the poor, the crippled, the lame, the blind, ¹⁴and you will be blessed. Although they cannot repay you, you will be repaid at the resurrection of the righteous'"* (Luke 14:12-14 NIV).

Rebecca Bryan-Howell

You hold a position of the highest honor as a representative of the Kingdom of Light. You have been entrusted with the riches of Heaven! Hang on to your crown because you have an enemy, Satan, who is waiting for an opportunity to steal it from you. He wants you to think that you can't do it, it's not worth it, you're missing out on the pleasures of life, and a plethora of other lies to keep you in the bog. Lift your vision, dearest, and feast your eyes on the goal, the good things of God and on Jesus, the Author and Finisher of your faith. Then your crown will stay intact, and your journey will be less of a battle and more of a blessing!

Pursue Excellence; it Looks Good on You

One of the surest ways to learn is to teach someone else, and your life is your podium! You have been chosen by God and appointed as His emissary. *"You didn't choose me. I chose you. I appointed you to go and produce lasting fruit, so that the Father will give you whatever you ask for, using my name"* (John 15:16 NLT). As Christ's ambassadors on earth, we speak for Him! *"So we are Christ's ambassadors; God is making his appeal through us. We speak for Christ when we plead, 'Come back to God!'"* (2 Corinthians 5:20 NLT). He has an important message for the world that He wants us to communicate. What kind of a diplomatic official sent by his country on a mission would relay his message and then add, "…but that's not *my* opinion. I think things should be entirely different." How long do you think he or she would keep their job if they misrepresented the ruler they had been hired to speak for?

Our mission is not only of the highest importance, but our position is one of power and influence. My dad used to say that true leaders are born, not made. There are many leadership skills that can be learned; but when someone is a born leader they are followed whether they lead for good or bad. Every gang of criminals has a leadership structure, and they are following their leaders to their destruction! You may not think of yourself as a born leader in the natural, but when you were born again in the spirit, you were born a

Born to Privilege

leader because people will follow the light within you. Shine bright and clear so that all who come behind you can see the path of excellence! *"But you are the chosen race, the King's priests, the holy nation, God's own people, chosen to proclaim the wonderful acts of God, who called you out of darkness into his own marvelous light"* (1 Peter 2:9 GNT).

In order to pursue excellence you need to be fully engaged in the process. When teaching ladies' Bible Study I used to start by writing the word "ENGAGE" on the whiteboard at the front of the class. I wanted the ladies in our group to have a mindset to focus on the subject and engage their minds in the material so that each one could find the takeaway that God had for their personal journey. I like the Berean Study Bible version of I Timothy 4:15 *"Be diligent in these matters and absorbed in them, so that your progress will be evident to all."* Have you heard the old slogan, "he went whole-hog"? It means to do something as completely as possible, holding nothing back. When someone is enthused to that level, everyone around them will know it. Your sisters in Christ will know it and the world around you will see that you are serious about God. Not only that, but God Himself will see your sincerity and reward it. I want to end this chapter with four components of pursuing excellence.

Seek: Get up and look. God promises us from Jeremiah 29:13, *"If you look for me wholeheartedly, you will find me"* (NLT). There is no fear of failure when we are seeking the Lord. He promises that our search will be rewarded! We can trust Him for flawless directions when we are searching for His Path of Life. There's nothing He loves more than having His children come to Him and ask, "What shall I do now?" Proverbs 3:5-6 has your answer: *"Trust in the LORD with all your heart; do not depend on your own understanding. ⁶Seek his will in all you do, and he will show you which path to take"* (NLT).

Plan: Choose a direction and trust the Lord to help you. These are two of my favorite verses to build confidence on the path of progress. *"You make known to me the path of life; you will fill me with joy in your presence, with eternal pleasures at your right hand"* (Psalm 16:11 NIV).

"The way of the righteous is like the first gleam of dawn, which shines ever brighter until the full light of day" (Proverbs 4:18 NLT). Not only can we expect joy and eternal pleasures all along the way, but the path will get brighter and easier to follow the farther we go! God makes our way perfect when our plan is to follow Him.

Do: Step out, trusting God to guide. We cannot be human and never experience doubt. Doubts will assail us from time to time, but we counter them with the truth of God's Word. The Psalmist taught us that our strength and security come from the Lord, and that through Him we can ascend heights that would be out of reach on our own. *"It is God who arms me with strength and keeps my way secure. ^{33}He makes my feet like the feet of a deer; he causes me to stand on the heights"* (Psalm 18:32-33 NIV). We can step out in many ways, too. Sometimes a door of opportunity will open and we can just step through. Other times the path may seem a bit foggy and we need to spend some time in prayer about our next step. We should regularly ask for confirmation about God's will, either through circumstances or through His Word to us. Often God will use the Scriptures to plainly answer the questions of life, as in Psalm 25:4-5, *"Show me the right path, O LORD; point out the road for me to follow .^{5}Lead me by your truth and teach me, for you are the God who saves me. All day long I put my hope in you"* (NLT).

By all means, remember and refer often to Psalm 37:23-24,*"The LORD directs the steps of the godly. He delights in every detail of their lives. ^{24}Though they stumble, they will never fall, for the LORD holds them by the hand"* (NLT). This is a good Scripture verse to post where you will see it often. You should know by this point in our study how much God loves you and what good things He has in store for your future; but on those hard days or long

Born to Privilege

nights it never hurts to remind yourself that He actually delights in every detail of your tiny, little life. He is with you all the way.

Press on: Keep moving forward; and don't look back. After being immersed in all the amazing stories of the Bible by my upbringing in Sunday School, I can't hardly hear the words "don't look back" without thinking of Lot's wife and how she turned to a pillar of salt! Looking back isn't helpful. You either end up pining for what you used to have or you get depressed about the mistakes you've made! We can't go back in time, but we can always go forward. God's mercies are new every morning and His rewards await our arrival at Life's finish line. *"I don't mean to say that I have already achieved these things or that I have already reached perfection. But I press on to possess that perfection for which Christ Jesus first possessed me. ¹³No, dear brothers and sisters, I have not achieved it, but I focus on this one thing: Forgetting the past and looking forward to what lies ahead, ¹⁴I press on to reach the end of the race and receive the heavenly prize for which God, through Christ Jesus, is calling us"* (Philippians 3:12-14 NLT). He wants us to run without fear of falling!

"I instruct you in the way of wisdom and lead you along straight paths. ¹²When you walk, your steps will not be hampered; when you run, you will not stumble" (Proverbs 4:11-12 NIV). We have a choice to make on our excellent journey: we get to decide which way to look and that will determine our progress, our safety, and our efficiency as we travel. I don't know where this powerful quote originated, but it has been used far and wide: "Fear looks back; Worry looks around; Faith looks up." So, ladies…what will it be?

Chapter Seven Summary

After today's chapter we could be tempted to have some dread dogging our steps because it sounds like a lot to wear the crown, even though we know it fits. We won't accept Dread, however, because we know that its twin is Worry and they are both in the Fear family which is, with all its members, diametrically opposed to

God, our King. We learned that Esther was a girl like us and that she conquered fear and excelled greatly for the times in which she lived, because she wore the crown that fit. Like Esther, we found that accepting our station was acting on our options; that it was a great honor to be positioned by the king and that the oath goes both ways: our Lord is as committed to us as we are to Him, and likely more so! We discovered to our relief that, in regard to our lives, "a cut above" was not about looking down on others but about living on higher ground and learning to lift others up as well. It was explained that we would have our challenges working with people while holding our standard, and that the key to balancing all the pieces would be waiting on the Lord and drawing life from that vine.

We learned a lot about Grace, as well as the tendency to be overly-accepting and tolerant of sinful behavior while trying to extend God's love and compassion to the sinner. We realized that the goal of love is not to keep people comfortable but to value their worth in God's eyes and lead them to Jesus, letting mercy and truth work together to meet all of their needs.

Then we went from how to carry others to how we must carry ourselves as Daughters of the King. We talked about deportment and the necessity of keeping our place with the dignity of God-given leadership so that we could be an example to the world; not only of a higher standard of living but of its rewards and benefits. We learned that our born-again experience puts us on an automatic leadership track to bring others to Jesus.

Now we know that our crown is something to hold onto and the way to do that is to live an honorable life with God's help. We learned what an honorable life looks like and how to develop and maintain those characteristics. Finally, we discussed the four aspects of pursuing excellence along with plenty of assurances from the Bible about God's faithfulness in helping us to run our race to win. We can choose where our focus will be, and that will

Born to Privilege

determine whether we will win or lose; but we want to win so we will choose Faith over Fear!

Theme Verse

Revelation 3:11 (NIV): *"I am coming soon. Hold on to what you have, so that no one will take your crown."*

Take-away Gems

- God has placed me on earth for such a time as this.
- My "station" is a God-given place of honor.
- I need time to be with the Lord and to listen to His guidance.
- I will extend grace to others because God has given grace to me.
- I trust God to enable me to embrace His standard.
- I choose to allow the Holy Spirit to govern my thoughts.
- God will help me to protect the honor He has entrusted to me.
- May all who come behind me, see Christ before me.
- When my heart seeks God, the pathway is bright.
- I choose to move forward in faith, instead of looking back in fear.

Own It!

Personalize: Review the Scripture passage in 2 Peter 1:3-11 under the subtitle, *Keepers of the Trust,* and make a list of the godly characteristics beginning with verse five. You should find nine of them. (Don't miss the "hard work ethic" in verse 10!) Then add to your list the four extra characteristics from the next few paragraphs. Which ones do you see yourself doing now? Is there room for improvement? Which characteristics do you want to develop? Do you believe God can form this part of His nature in you? Let the Holy Spirit show you how to begin.

Ponder: Write down your take-away gems for Chapter Seven in your journal or notebook. Choose your personal nugget for this chapter, either from your gems list or from elsewhere in the text, and write something about why you chose this concept. During your quiet time ask the Holy Spirit to help you identify the character traits He wants you to develop at this stage of your life.

Pursue: Decide how you can exercise determination in building godly character. Choose one character trait from your list above that you would like to pursue and write it in your journal. Look up the word in a dictionary and write down a concise definition beside it. Then do a simple Bible study about it using your Bible concordance, a Bible dictionary, or online Bible study tools. If this is new to you, great! Ask for tips from your leader or in your Circle of Wagons group. You are showing determination by learning something new! Stretch those unused muscles and go for it!

Persist: Write out the theme verse for Chapter Seven on a 3 x 5 card in the Bible version of your choice. Post it wherever you can see it often! Remember that hiding these verses in your heart and reviewing them in your mind will help you to learn to think like God does. Bringing your thoughts in line with the mind of Christ will enable you to become all that you were created to be! If the *Pursue* section above seemed overwhelming to you, break it into small steps and take them on one at a time as you are able. Any progress is better than "sitting against the curb"! You can do it!

Partner: In your Circle of Wagons, talk about what 'wearing your crown' and 'accepting your station' means in everyday life. Discuss the character traits, which ones you understand and the ones you want to know more about. Help each other with tips on how to be more determined in pursuing these things. Find someone in your group who wants to pursue the same trait that you are working on, and talk about ways to hold each other accountable in your progress.

Chapter 8: Royal Counsel – New Normal

Chapter Seven was tough. How many times have you heard the phrase, "I think he bit off more than he could chew"? Better yet, how many times have you said it about yourself when you started something new only to become completely overwhelmed by its magnitude within the first few days or hours? Here's another common assessment: "I don't think she knew what she was getting into." So, did you know what you were getting into by choosing to become a disciple of Christ? Or did you come across some things in the last chapter that made you wonder if there was much more to wearing this crown than you first supposed? Though the crown fits, does it suddenly feel quite a bit heavier than it did when you first came into the Kingdom of Light?

I've always been amazed by the cultures of the world where women carry huge pots of water or tall stacks of stuff on their heads; not only for long distances, but often without needing their hands to balance the load! Even more amazing is the way they walk along as if they don't give it a second thought; like it isn't even there! That is a skill that I will never master unless Pot-Carrier I is a class I am involuntarily signed up for in Heaven! For now, though, let's consider two things that bring this rabbit trail back around.

First, even if our crown was that heavy, we could learn to carry our heads high and keep our balance because this skill is learned. Those amazing women are taught from a very young age to carry their burdens carefully and most efficiently for success; if they can

Born to Privilege

learn that, we could, too! Secondly, we've already learned the best way to carry our burdens: give them to the Lord and count them as blessings! These two strategies make any load in life significantly lighter! We don't carry ourselves with poise and grace by physical skills we have developed, but by the spiritual power that resides within our being through Christ, our King. When we are weak, He is strong; and that is why we can do all things through Christ, including the responsibilities that come with our status as Daughters of God. We are well able to walk as royalty, carry out His standards, and keep the trust He has bestowed upon us, His cherished ones.

From Now On

This Bible study has brought us down a path of amazing discovery. We have learned who we really are and why we are actually here! Now it is time to move on with the treasure trove that we have found; this endless and eternal collection of valuables with which we have been so generously endowed by our Creator.

As we journey through life, we will have countless opportunities to compare our new gold standard of living with the ever-changing "normal" of the world around us. In your own life time, whether you are young or old, you should be able to look back and see a plethora of changes from "how it used to be". The definitions of family, authority, respect and honor have all taken a dive! What about truth? We live by the one with a capital 'T', but the world doesn't see truth like that. Morals and decency, marriage and divinity lie across the world's landscape like a dog-leg railroad track that has been warped by weather changes and shifting ground. When this happens on a section of rail serious accidents can ensue. As a retired railroad conductor, my husband has seen many a mangled heap of cars thrown from the track due to these sleeping antagonists. In fact, his own life was on the line several times when these unexpected derailments happened on his watch, due to no fault of his own or his crew.

Our profession is very similar in this way. As people of God, we are traveling an unpredictable track, dangerously affected by the landscape and elements of the world we travel through. Wisdom calls us to be vigilant and pay attention to the routes we follow so that our own journey is not altered by these fatal flaws. Keeping to the standard of the Kingdom will prevent derails and pile-ups along the way that would set us back indefinitely or halt progress by random hurdles tossed across our course as we run the race.

Kingdom Culture

We would do well to think of the Christian life as a culture of its own with valuable customs and characteristics worth protecting. Most cultures of people groups worldwide have a code of honor that implies generational adherence to this patriotic mindset. Customs and traditions that are held sacred and dear are passed down from generation to generation so that thousands of years later we can still identify certain cultures by their fundamental structure of family and community values, language, foods, religions and governing practices. Christianity is a culture all its own that goes across racial and ethnic[23] boundaries, yet holds to certain values, traditions, practices, living standards, and authority structures that should be cherished and protected for the good of all. Our standard was created by God, and is a set of "best practices" – if you will – for the success of His followers and of His ultimate purpose for mankind. As my husband often says, "We are a part of *God's* plan; He is not a part of ours." Furthermore, we don't have to worry about that standard changing with every passing persuasion or social philosophy. We have the confidence that our God is unchangeable. The Bible makes this element of His supernatural nature very clear: *"God is not human, that he should lie, not a human being, that he should change his mind. Does he speak and then not act? Does he promise and not fulfill?"* (Numbers 23:19 NIV). Also, in Hebrews 6:17-19: *"God also bound himself with an oath, so that those who received the promise could be perfectly sure*

---

[23] Emma Bryce, "What's the Difference between Race and Ethnicity?" LiveScience, February 8, 2020, https://www.livescience.com/difference-between-race-ethnicity.html

Born to Privilege

that he would never change his mind. ¹⁸So God has given both his promise and his oath. These two things are unchangeable because it is impossible for God to lie. Therefore, we who have fled to him for refuge can have great confidence as we hold to the hope that lies before us. ¹⁹This hope is a strong and trustworthy anchor for our souls. It leads us through the curtain into God's inner sanctuary" (NLT). We have a creed we can count on to stand the test of time.

Remember Who You Are

We can ask ourselves, or others in our Circle of Wagons, what it means to be part of God's plan but we already know. That's what we've been studying these past weeks in the pages of our book, Born to Privilege. We have learned that being born again into the Kingdom of Light is more than asking the simple question, "Got Jesus?" He is not an item to add to our already full lives, like that priceless bottle of water that we stuff into our backpack before a long hike. Jesus is not a passing encounter, but a person with whom we develop an ongoing relationship that grows and deepens over time. Salvation is not an experience, but a whole new way of life that changes and grows every day. We are on a new pathway that is taking us to exciting and fulfilling places. So, let's do a quick review of our identity.

We have a new life. Our old life within the world system of values has been shucked off and left behind because it is of little value to us now. *"He died for everyone so that those who receive his new life will no longer live for themselves. Instead, they will live for Christ, who died and was raised for them. ¹⁶So we have stopped evaluating others from a human point of view. At one time we thought of Christ merely from a human point of view. How differently we know him now! ¹⁷This means that anyone who belongs to Christ has become a new person. The old life is gone; a new life has begun!"* (2 Corinthians 5:15-17 NLT).

We have a new nature. Colossians 3:10 tells us, *"Put on your new nature, and be renewed as you learn to know your Creator and become like him"* (NLT). When you have a favorite old sweater that you just can't let go and then you finally find a beautiful new item that fits perfectly, it's an easy trade! Suddenly your worn and faded ball of fuzz doesn't feel so cozy and irreplaceable anymore. We have new clothes in God's kingdom. *"Since you have heard about Jesus and have learned the truth that comes from him, ²²throw off your old sinful nature and your former way of life, which is corrupted by lust and deception. ²³Instead, let the Spirit renew your thoughts and attitudes. ²⁴Put on your new nature, created to be like God—truly righteous and holy"* (Ephesians 4:21-24 NLT).

We have been given a new name, a new purpose, a whole new identity! In fact, it goes deeper than that, we have a new bloodline and royalty courses through our veins. *"But to all who believed him and accepted him, he gave the right to become children of God. ¹³They are reborn—not with a physical birth resulting from human passion or plan, but a birth that comes from God"* (John 1:12-13 NLT). We have also been given the mind of Christ (1 Corinthians 2:16) and our minds are being renewed day by day (Colossians 3:10).

We are not limited to earthly decay. *"For this reason we never become discouraged. Even though our physical being is gradually decaying, yet our spiritual being is renewed day after day. ¹⁷And this small and temporary trouble we suffer will bring us a tremendous and eternal glory, much greater than the trouble. ¹⁸For we fix our attention, not on things that are seen, but on things that are unseen. What can be seen lasts only for a time, but what cannot be seen lasts forever"* (2 Corinthians 4:16-18 GNT).

We have been planted in a new culture, and received assignments for our new mission. *"But you are a chosen people, a royal priesthood, a holy nation, a people for God's own possession, to proclaim the virtues of Him who called you out of darkness into His marvelous light"* (1 Peter 2:9 BSB).

Born to Privilege

Best of all, we have been provided with all the tools, equipment, and supplies to make our mission a successful one! *"By his divine power, God has given us everything we need for living a godly life. We have received all of this by coming to know him, the one who called us to himself by means of his marvelous glory and excellence. ⁴And because of his glory and excellence, he has given us great and precious promises. These are the promises that enable you to share his divine nature and escape the world's corruption caused by human desires"* (2 Peter 1:3-4 NLT).

We need never be loners again because we are a part of something bigger than ourselves and bigger than this world. Take a look at this: *"Now these are the gifts Christ gave to the church: the apostles, the prophets, the evangelists, and the pastors and teachers. ¹²Their responsibility is to equip God's people to do his work and build up the church, the body of Christ. ¹³This will continue until we all come to such unity in our faith and knowledge of God's Son that we will be mature in the Lord, measuring up to the full and complete standard* of *Christ. ¹⁴Then we will no longer be immature like children. We won't be tossed and blown about by every wind of new teaching. We will not be influenced when people try to trick us with lies so clever they sound like the truth. ¹⁵Instead, we will speak the truth in love, growing in every way more and more like Christ, who is the head of his body, the church. ¹⁶He makes the whole body fit together perfectly. As each part does its own special work, it helps the other parts grow, so that the whole body is healthy and growing and full of love"* (Ephesians 4:11-16 NLT).

We are done being lost and tossed around. We don't ever have to be tricked, lied to and held back again. We are connected to the Vine of Christ and we each have a special part to play as valuable members of His body, the church. We have learned that we can't do life alone, and that "together" is the culture of God's kingdom. Now our job is to keep our eye on the prize and keep moving. No looking back!

Rebecca Bryan-Howell

Shutting Out the Voices

In Chapter Six, "Dressed for Battle", we learned that a Daughter of God (princess, if you please) can – and must – wear her tiara and her combat boots at the same time! We learned that it's a battle out there and we are already on the winning side. We also discovered that this world system we've been talking about is Satan's domain (for now) and that he is the arch enemy of our Savior and King! Since this is the case, we are surrounded by the patterns, perspectives, preferences and philosophies of the world. Consequently, one of our primary responsibilities is to sort out these voices that swirl around us, and to separate truth from error.

What does the voice of the world sound like? We hear it every day in the news media, secular education, politics, and societal pursuits. For that reason none of us should have difficulty in defining or describing it. What we need to focus on more is how it measures up to God's standard, since that's the one we are now living by! *"For the sinful nature is always hostile to God. It never did obey God's laws, and it never will. [8]That's why those who are still under the control of their sinful nature can never please God"* (Romans 8:7-8 NLT). This next verse tells us why: *"Since they thought it foolish to acknowledge God, he abandoned them to their foolish thinking and let them do things that should never be done"* (Romans 1:28 NLT); and the verses following that describe it in detail. This is a challenging assignment because, don't forget, God's children are still human. As our dedication to the Lord deepens and we grow to maturity in our Christian lifestyle it will become much easier. Right now, however, the world may be saying some things that still sound plausible, even agreeable, to us. They may be doing some things that we still have ties to – through close relationships we have with others, or activities and perceptions we are drawn to in some way because of our old fleshly nature calling us back. This is where we have to decide to cut the ties with the old, shabby sweater and actively put on that new nature! We have to use our free will to choose God's standard

Born to Privilege

every day over the voice of the world that yammers in our ears continually. We have to practice, and thereby learn, to reach for the harder right instead of the easier wrong.

What does the voice of reason sound like? It can include human logic, tangible facts and figures, proven formulas, accepted theories, and worldly wisdom – as in philosophies that are born out of academic studies and examinations of thought systems, concepts, and mortal realities. Let's look at logic. This voice can be a tricky one because the world we live in calls it "common sense" which none of us wants to be without! The dictionary defines logic as a sensible or rational argument or thought, rather than one that is driven by whim or emotion. That sounds good, right? It's about proven patterns, conclusive evidence, and interactions that have inevitable consequences. For instance, the statement, "If you jump off a cliff you will fall down," is not just a theory. We can speculate all we want to that our bodies could possibly move up or to the side; but no matter how sincerely we believe that we have other options, down is actually the only consequence to cliff-jumping.

Now, let's take something that is not quite so obvious, with consequences not as firm as that of the Law of Gravity. I want to bake a beautiful dessert for my dinner party and I've found a recipe online that will be perfect. I have all the ingredients and instructions for my three-layer Coco-Mocha Crème Torte. Preparation time is 30 minutes and bake time is 25. Cooling and assembly are 40 minutes more so I'm excited to try this! I can have it on my cake server in the fridge in an hour and a half! But I'm not considering the fact that a Betsy Homemaker professional cook who had everything in its place and at her fingertips recorded these time allowances. So, first, I can't find my measuring cups because my dear, helpful hubby put the clean dishes away last. Then it takes longer than expected to crush the graham crackers and chop the nuts. In my already rushed mental state I have to use hard butter and cream cheese because I forgot to take them out to soften ahead of time! Now I'm discouraged because, even if the rest of the process goes like a happy dream I'm still 45 minutes behind schedule. Needless to say, with the clock ticking loudly and every second bouncing off the walls of my kitchen into my vulnerable ears, the cooling process is crowded by my impatience and by the time all the layers are frosted and neatly stacked they begin to slide on my perfect frosting which is now slightly-melted. Leaning precariously to one side, my finished product looks nothing like the picture…and I can forget the garnish because that is definitely not happening! You're laughing because you've been there! What we forgot to include in our planning was room for variables – the biggest one being me! We can work with these scenarios and laugh with our friends about the dessert tasting much better than it looks, yet that "proven" recipe just turned into a presumptuous, man-made theory! We have to conclude that one person's reliable formula, proven by thorough testing, can still become a disaster for someone else. Recipes, medications, and facial products can all work perfect for you while turning me into a monster because of the variables from person to person.

So let's talk philosophy. Peoples and cultures act according to the underlying precepts, beliefs and principles that have developed throughout human history. Our interactions with the elements of our world, its kingdoms and its sciences, together with human consciousness, experience, history, relationship, religion and more have established schools of thought that frame our knowledge and understanding for life. But the Bible has a lot to say about knowledge, and there are two different kinds: the knowledge of the world and the knowledge of God. The philosophies of the world, although often influenced by various religious concepts, are still hollow and deceptive; hollow because they are missing the core of Truth, which comes from God, and deceptive for two reasons. One, any spiritual elements thrown into the mix will likely come from the world's many religions that are entirely man-made and have nothing to do with the God of the Universe, and are thereby a ruse. Two, these philosophies often include elements of Truth that we already believe but are mixed with other ingredients that are flatly false, ruining the whole batch! When we hear something that we

Born to Privilege

believe to be true, the ears of our soul perk up enough to crack the door open and listen a little more. The problem is that we can be drawn into worldly philosophies by the bait of truth and make ourselves vulnerable to bad information and a spirit of confusion. That's why it's so important to have the Spirit of God within us to activate discernment that will help us preserve the Truth while closing the door on bad philosophy. God knew we would be faced with a lot of compromised information along our earthly pathway and He addresses it in His basic instruction book for life, the Bible. First of all, He clearly tells us that we will see things in the world that look good but are not! Proverbs 14:12 warns us that *"There is a way that appears to be right, but in the end it leads to death"* (NIV). Later, in the New Testament epistles, Colossians 2:8 instructs us further, *"See to it that no one takes you captive through hollow and deceptive philosophy, which depends on human tradition and the elemental spiritual forces of this world rather than on Christ"* (NIV). This verse reminds us of that God-shaped hole within every human heart – and therefore, inherent in any human thinking that is void of the Holy Spirit's influence; because the world has its own spiritual element that is very real and very dark. This spirit of the world likes to masquerade as reliable truth but, like the poisoned apple that hides its deadly venom behind a shiny skin, it leads to death. (See 2 Corinthians 11:14).

Pure Truth

In this chapter we are talking about things that are different now that we know who we are and why we are here. God has provided us with pure Truth and reliable instructions and guidelines for getting through life successfully. His salvation package is complete; we don't need anything from a world that doesn't know Him or understand His ways. 1 Corinthians 2:12-14 explains, *"What we have received is not the spirit of the world, but the Spirit who is from God, so that we may understand what God has freely given us. ^{13}This is what we speak, not in words taught us by human wisdom but in words taught by the Spirit, explaining spiritual realities with Spirit-taught words. ^{14}The person without the Spirit* *does not accept the things that come from the Spirit of God but considers them foolishness, and cannot understand them because they are discerned only through the Spirit"* (NIV). Here God is telling us that our human hearts and minds are not capable on their own of understanding everything we need to know. Without the indwelling of the Holy Spirit we cannot understand God or His ways. In fact, our human hearts alone will lead us astray. Consider this startling fact: *"The heart is deceitful above all things, and desperately wicked: who can know it"* (Jeremiah 17:9 KJV)? Wow...our human heart is not only incapable of understanding spiritual truth, but quite willing to purposefully deceive us into pursuing evil. The influence of the Holy Spirit that sweeps in when we make the conscious decision to repent of our sin and follow Christ is our only hope of ever learning and understanding this miraculous Truth that makes us a new creation and gives us entry into God's eternal kingdom.

We've talked about human logic, man-made theories, and worldly philosophies that can only be properly dissected by the Spirit of Truth. These, plus the attitudes of our own deceitful hearts are the voices we have to learn to sort out and analyze by God's standard of Truth. We know that the voice of the Lord is completely reliable; but how do we recognize His voice? In all of our sorting out, can we easily learn to distinguish the one voice that we need to hear from all the others that clamor so loudly?

My Sheep Hear My Voice

The above discussion about the demanding voices of the world around us seems to depict the spawning of a cacophony not unlike a pack of hungry hounds baying at the helpless raccoon cornered on a high tree branch. How interesting, therefore, that the biblical answer lands squarely and simply before us. *"I am the good shepherd: I know my own sheep, and they know me"* (John 10:14 NLT). Later in verses 27-29 of that same chapter Christ continues, *"My sheep hear My voice, and I know them, and they follow Me;* [28]*and I give eternal life to them, and they will never perish; and*

Born to Privilege

no one will snatch them out of My hand. ²⁹My Father, who has given them to Me, is greater than all; and no one is able to snatch them out of the Father's hand." (NAS) The Amplified Bible brings it right into the present, *"The sheep that are my own hear and are listening to my voice."*

Although it is happening more and more these days, it is not common to hear the audible voice of God in our finite, human ears. Yet He has given us other ways to listen, namely, His words to live by in the Holy Bible; and if we are serious about knowing what He is saying to us, we will read it daily and ponder its instruction with the intention of applying these principles to our lives. Additionally, as we discussed in Chapter Three, we also have that gentle but prevailing voice of the Holy Spirit, the Comforter whom Jesus promised to send when He ascended to the right hand of His Father in heaven. Jesus explained that his Holy Spirit would not only be our constant teacher and guide through this life, but that He would also grant us access to power we would need to overcome every obstacle in our way. This power is also – and I quote from Chapter Three again – "a thick layer of supernatural protection against spiritual contamination, which will come at us from a variety of different sources," including the voices of the world. So learning to listen to this now prevailing, yet gentle and sweet, voice inside our spirit is the best and most accessible resource for hearing God clearly, above the din.

Let's Talk "Normal"

We live in a world that has a million different definitions for the word 'normal' and likes it that way! The dictionary definition for the general use of the word says, "Conforming to the standard or the common type; usual; not abnormal; regular; natural" or "serving to establish a standard". Okay, that's interesting since everybody seems to have their own standard these days. We often hear the question, "What's normal, anyway?" with the accepted conclusion that my normal is expected to be different from your normal. Yet, in Psychology, the scientific study of the mind and behavior, normal is still defined as "Approximately average in any psychological trait, as intelligence, personality, or emotional adjustment;" and "free from any mental disorder; sane." We are more likely to accept a norm in these fields because nobody wants to claim insanity as 'normal' even though we have picked up common phrases such as, "that's insane; but she's just crazy!" As if to say that crazy or insane behavior is an accepted choice, we have turned that 'taboo' and the questionable into a normal option or personality trait. There was a time in our recent past that most people would confidently state the obvious, "That's not natural"; but now we often dump the words 'natural', 'average', 'normal', 'usual', 'standard', and even 'insane' into the general category of subjective opinion which changes continually from person to person!

If we are doing, saying, or thinking something that we don't want to change, our amoral society allows us to confidently state, "This is normal for me." However, before we let it go, let's look at the part of the definition regarding Biology and the medical field. Here, 'normal' means: "Free from any infection or other form of disease or malformation, or from experimental therapy or manipulation;" or "of natural occurrence." [24]

Ah, now we are getting somewhere because though society in general may demand the freedom to choose their own 'normal' in attitude and behavior, they will not be so likely to accept a cancerous growth or a bulging disc in their physical body as 'natural'! In fact, most people understand what is or is not a 'natural occurrence' in their physical body. Hence, upon discovering an infection, disease, or malformation in our bodies, it is 'normal' to become alarmed or concerned about the consequences of ignoring these things. Rather than accepting them as par for the course and allowing them to develop, we will consult our medical professionals as soon as possible to see how the 'abnormal' condition can be remedied!

---

[24] "Normal," Dictionary.com, https://www.dictionary.com/browse/normal

The discrepancy between these two trains of thought is neatly hidden in the big 'I'. Whenever something becomes uncomfortable for us, we often – speaking of humans in general – change our definitions to fit our wishes or to produce our desired outcomes. We are unwilling to consider the fact that, as beings created in God's image, we have normal functions of the body, the soul, and the spirit that are meant to work smoothly together, helping us to do and think and be all that we were created for. This entire study has been about recognizing what God intended for us in contrast to what we know, have experienced thus far, or have been made to believe through the voices and philosophies of the world we live in. And we have discovered that the abundant life that God promises to His children is very different from a life lived without this knowledge. We have seen, beyond a shadow of doubt, that God's 'normal' and the world's 'normal' are diametrically opposed to one another!

Let's dissect that statement a bit further. How does the world define 'normal', aside from the fact that everybody wants to choose their own? The last paragraph began with the big 'I'; the Me Factor. We have been programmed with statements such as, "It's my life;" "That's just ME;" "Everybody's different, and this is me;" "I'm OK, you're OK;" "It is what it is;" "I have a right to choose;" "This is what I deserve;" and many others. Our pursuits line up with whatever makes us happy in relationships, possessions, education, career and retirement, activities, entertainment and more. The world is full of opportunities! This is the outer limit; now let's move in one layer to 'up-close-and-personal'. How do you personally define 'normal'? How do you see it, or believe it should be, in your work, your family, your health, at home, at church, or in your interaction with society in general? How do you define normal feelings, normal expectations, and the like? This is a good discussion because sometimes we need an up-close reminder of where our thoughts have been taking us and what mindsets we have developed over time.

Now let's get to the center, the inner layer, the heart of the matter. By this point in our study, you know exactly what I mean; the eternal part of you that is currently housed in this temporary shell called the human body. Remember when we talked about the understanding and ability of walking in two realms at the same time? This is where we reviewed our peculiar status as spiritual beings living and walking on a physical earth. That part of our study in Chapter Three defines your spirit as, "the part of you that communicates with God, your creator, and interacts with that supernatural realm of the spirit where eternal realities take precedence over our finite human existence". The tragic element of the world's view of life is the missing connection that makes life worth living; the God Factor. Notice here that I did not say, 'the spiritual factor' because our discussion in Chapter Six explained that our world is chock-full of spiritual entities and experiences that would draw us into the deceptions of our arch enemy, Satan, whose sole purpose is to rob us of our God-ordained destinies. People seeking a random spiritual experience might get anything from a fairy garden of chums to a fiendish garrison of creepy captors! Satan is no respecter of costumes when he comes to entrap us with his lies. That's why it is so important for us to study the Truth God has provided so that we can automatically recognize those enticing side-roads and unexpected trap-doors, however brightly they may be decorated. The only reliable spiritual experience is the one with Jesus Christ in the center. With that as our precedent, we can move on to our final question: What is God's definition of normal?

Your New Normal

There are three foundational elements of our new normal as the Daughters of God. The first goes back to the catalyst of the Christian faith that sets it apart from other religions. It's all about relationship; not a set of rules or a creed packed with impossible ideals. Our faith is built upon our relationship to the Savior of our souls; the Author and Finisher of this amazing journey; the King of the Universe and beyond where we will spend eternity with Him as citizens of the Kingdom of Light. We don't have to wonder if we have done enough good deeds to get us into some utopian dreamworld, or struggle through a system of foggy symbols and rituals displayed by mystical gurus and purported to please a spiritual despot we can never relate to. We know the Savior of the World, and we stay in the Truth by sticking with Him! In 1 John 2:27 the apostle John reminds us how this works: *"But you have received the Holy Spirit, and he lives within you, so you don't need anyone to teach you what is true. For the Spirit teaches you everything you need to know, and what he teaches is true—it is not a lie. So just as he has taught you, remain in fellowship with Christ"* (NLT). We are not restricted by any social, ecclesiastical, or meritorious barriers to keep us from growing that friendship as quickly as we desire. Sinners who come to Christ through faith and repentance, and acknowledge Him as Lord, are instantly saints; saved by grace and given new life. Not perfect, but forgiven and renewable! We can walk with Him every moment of every day at will, continually discovering the riches we share as heirs of His kingdom. It's more than relationship; it's relationship with reward!

The second foundational element of our new normal is this new life that is ours through this relationship with Christ, our Lord. With our salvation from sin and destruction comes a whole new plane of purposeful living. We were not only born to be found and saved by Him, but to be agents of His will and purpose on this earth. The exciting part is that everything we need to complete this path He has set before us is already provided! (2 Peter 1:3-10) The more we dig into our new life the more of it we will want to know and experience. We will join with the saints who have gone before us in living their lives for God, and we'll identify with David's full confidence in Psalm 16:11, *"You will show me the way of life, granting me the joy of your presence and the pleasures of living with you forever"* (NLT). As you reach for God's instruction and choose His paths, you will experience the results of ingesting His words, as in Proverbs 1:3 *"Their purpose is to teach people to live disciplined and successful lives, to help them do what is right, just, and fair"* (NLT). The more you engage in following His ways the stronger your hunger for truth will become, and you will look forward eagerly to gathering up all the nuggets for nourishing a strong and healthy lifestyle. What's more, no one can take it away, by any means, at any time.

As I write this chapter, the world is experiencing something that many of us have heard about but never seen in our lifetime; a pandemic called COVID-19. It is a manmade virus that was hatched in a laboratory and leaked to the world. Millions of people have been infected and thousands have died across the globe, from the richest and most prosperous nations to the poorest of countries. Pestilence has no particular preference in victims. Many stores have empty shelves, travel has been interrupted, all businesses that are not considered vital for survival are closed, and those who are not quarantined with this illness have at least some form of restrictive order from their government to shelter in place and stay out of public places whenever possible in order to stop the spread of this virus. It's hard to believe. Particularly in a country as free as America, this kind of restriction is both foreign and unsettling. The rumor mill is running hot, of course, and the internet is overflowing with conspiracy theorists spouting their views about what all of this means and what will happen next. The fact is, it is mid-April and we are barely six weeks into the effects of this pandemic. We have not likely seen the worst of it yet, nor can we presume what the future will hold, though predictions are grim. God's people understand that he informs His prophets about what He is going to do in the earth, but the mixture of speculation and human reasoning has stirred the pot until it is hard to discern the meat from the goulash! Still, when it all subsides we will look back and see that God's Word did not change and His promises remained true.

Do you realize the powerful assurance nestled into Psalm 23? Verse one declares, *"The LORD is my shepherd; I have all that I need"* (NLT). This is the power for living that I have sought to embed into my message throughout the chapters of this book. It's not just a slight wave of the hand that says, "No worries, you're okay." Rather, these words are staples in the diet of life for all who belong to the Lord. Nothing is too hard for Him, and whether our

Born to Privilege

circumstances deliver pinto beans or Petit fours He will use the menu for our good. The entire Psalm is rich with treasures but for the purpose of our immediate subject I want to go to verse five. *"You prepare a feast for me in the presence of my enemies."* This means that when we sit at His table we will do more than barely survive; He provides a feast that cannot be stolen or minimized in the face of any difficulty or enemy invasion – physical or spiritual. When we are surrounded by worries and fears, by anomalies that rock our world – things that are not normal – His provisions never diminish, His delicacies remain plentiful, and His copious care still surrounds our quaking hearts. You are safe in His arms.

You can find plenty of pretty language in this book as you read the analogous comparisons between our life on earth and our position in Christ. You may love or loathe the tiaras, the riches, the promises and the privileges we have used to paint our features as Daughters of God with a purely spiritual heritage. You may have equally loved or loathed the part of the equation that corresponds to our earthly pilgrimage; the burdens we must bear, the sacrifices made, the patience to endure hardships and the challenges we must overcome as part of the responsibility of our crown. These descriptions of our life in both realms can seem surreal, yet there is no greater reality, and no greater mystery than how God has ordained these two planes to blend and converge in the accomplishment of His will. We are a privileged lot, as bearers of the Light, and every aspect of this calling is as real and important as the others that make us who we are, both in this world and in the world to come; speaking of which, the third foundational element of our new normal is the anticipation of Christ's triumphant return for His Bride, the Church.

From the time I was a small child we were taught through Scripture, Bible stories, and music to watch for the return of Christ Jesus, our King! We used to sing an old hymn, a favorite through many generations of Christians, "When the Roll is Called up Yonder", that said it plainly.

Rebecca Bryan-Howell

> *"When the trumpet of the Lord shall sound,*
> *and time shall be no more*
> *And the morning breaks, eternal, bright and fair.*
> *When the saved of earth shall gather*
> *over on the other shore,*
> *And the roll is called up yonder, I'll be there."*[25]

Only the first few lines are quoted here, but the whole of this song echoed the truth of Christ's second coming found in scriptural studies of the subject and was one of my earliest exposures to this exhilarating doctrinal principle of the Christian faith. *"But let me reveal to you a wonderful secret. We will not all die, but we will all be transformed!* [52]*It will happen in a moment, in the blink of an eye, when the last trumpet is blown. For when the trumpet sounds, those who have died will be raised to live forever. And we who are living will also be transformed"* (1 Corinthians 15:51-52 NLT).

Jesus is coming again to rule on this earth as Lord of lords and King of kings, as the Bible exhorts us to look forward to. It also warns us that the condition of our earth before the Christ's return will be dark and dire; and that we will need to encourage one another to watch for these signs and remain diligent to our mission until then. *"When the Son of Man returns, it will be like it was in Noah's day.* [38]*In those days before the flood, the people were enjoying banquets and parties and weddings right up to the time Noah entered his boat.* [39]*People didn't realize what was going to happen until the flood came and swept them all away. That is the way it will be when the Son of Man comes.* [40]*Two men will be working together in the field; one will be taken, the other left.* [41]*Two women will be grinding flour at the mill; one will be taken, the other left.* [42]*So you, too, must keep watch! For you don't know what day your Lord is coming"* (Matthew 24:37-42 NLT).

The book of Revelation was given by God to the apostle, John, during his banishment on the Isle of Patmos by the Roman

---

[25] James Milton Black, "When the Roll is Called up Yonder," 1893, Public Domain, https://songselect.ccli.com/Songs/31315

Born to Privilege

government. The first few verses of chapter one tell us that God gave it to him to show us, the followers of Christ, the events that will take place before Christ returns to rule the earth. There is a spiritual blessing that comes to those who read The Revelation, and it is also an imperative message to tuck deep in our hearts so that as these things come to fruition we will recognize them.

"This is a revelation from Jesus Christ, which God gave him to show his servants the events that must soon take place. He sent an angel to present this revelation to his servant John; ²who faithfully reported everything he saw. This is his report of the Word of God and the testimony of Jesus Christ. ³God blesses the one who reads the words of this prophecy to the church, and he blesses all who listen to its message and obey what it says, for the time is near" (Revelation 1:1-3 NLT).

Remember when we talked about the many religions of our world, and the importance of studying the Truth so that we could easily recognize error when it presented itself in various forms? This is the same concept we need to use for The Revelation. It is full of mystery and spiritual symbolism, but it is Truth and we need to be familiar with it. Many people feel that, since they can't understand it or apply much of it to their daily lives, it is a book to be "kept on the shelf", so to speak. Don't be blinded by this indifferent, yet popular, attitude! The Revelation is as vital a part of the Holy Bible as any of your favorite books in the canon of Scripture. Reading it often will not only instruct and edify you with its invaluable end time message, but will serve to familiarize you with the mysterious details that will be fully revealed in due time as these events begin to happen on earth and in the heavens.

When we are traveling across the country to an unfamiliar destination, we rely on highway signs along the way to assure us that we are on the right road, or that we are coming closer to our destination. The more we travel a particular road, the more familiar we become with the points along the route and the easier it is to get our bearings and keep track of our progress. Familiarity with the map fosters peace and confidence because even if we hit a storm or a section of road construction we still know where we are, and where we are going. This is the same condition that God wants us to be in during our spiritual journey. If God has truly given us all we need for this life, which He has (2 Peter 1:3), then we should never experience the kind of confusion that throws us so far off course that we cannot find our way back. We may take the wrong exit or make a wrong turn, but we have the map and can always get back on track to our destinations in God.

"This letter is from John to the seven churches in the province of Asia. Grace and peace to you from the one who is, who always was, and who is still to come; from the sevenfold Spirit before his throne; ⁵and from Jesus Christ. He is the faithful witness to these things, the first to rise from the dead, and the ruler of all the kings of the world. All glory to him who loves us and has freed us from our sins by shedding his blood for us. ⁶He has made us a Kingdom of priests for God his Father. All glory and power to him forever and ever! Amen.
⁷Look! He comes with the clouds of heaven; and everyone will see him—even those who pierced him. And all the nations of the world will mourn for him. Yes! Amen!
⁸"'I am the Alpha and the Omega—the beginning and the end,' says the Lord God. 'I am the one who is, who always was, and who is still to come—the Almighty One'" (Revelation 1:4-8 NLT).

Read The Revelation, ladies! Read it until you can hear those words of mystery with interest and anticipation instead of confusion or dread. A good way to take in truths that you don't fully understand is to pray as you read, "Thank you, Lord, for revealing your truth to me; and providing the understanding that I need exactly when I need it!"

The letter that John wrote to the churches of Asia so many years ago is just as important for the church today, and will continue to be vital instruction to the worldwide Body of Christ until we are all

Born to Privilege

sharing that glorious heavenly kingdom with our Lord and Savior in Eternity.

Chapter Eight Summary

Well, girls; this wraps it up. In this study we realized that we had been born to privilege, and were qualified for some great benefits that we didn't know enough about. We've been gathering together to learn about all these things in a hands on classroom where we have seen, heard, touched and tasted a passel of truths that were there all the time, just waiting for us to dig into. Each week we had time to personalize them; and we took them home to ponder, pursue them further and partner with others who were on the same track. It's been rich, enlightening, and rewarding.

Now, in our final chapter, we have been provided with empty backpacks (with plenty of glam, naturally!) All of our new provisions are sitting around us and it is time to pack them up and hit the road. It was fun to get new goodies every week; to talk about them and touch them and know that they were ours to keep. Now we get to travel with them. Do we want to? Does it sober us a bit to leave the company of the Princess Corp and get started on our new and personal path of privilege as a full-fledged Daughter of God?

We are going out these doors with a New Normal; one that God has ordained. We are entering a new chapter of our lives that God will be heavily contributing to. We have learned that our lives were limited before and, now that God has edited our plot, the pages ahead will be much more colorful and adventurous. We won't ever have to be stuck in 'writer's block' again because our source of material just got a lot bigger. New nature, new name, new purpose, new pathway; we are prepped and ready for our new destiny in God. We have the voice of The Good Shepherd to guide us and His presence to go with us all the way, as well as our Circle of Wagons to share each phase of the journey with us.

Rebecca Bryan-Howell

Never Look Back

As we come to the end of our study, I urge you as Daughters of God who are to partake in the riches of His kingdom to remember the importance of this last chapter. Life is full of changes; you have had some already and you will have more. Things will happen that will mess up your 'normal' and require you to make decisions about how to proceed. The difference is that you don't have to dread it anymore. Remember that God's normal will always balance and beautify your life. His counsel is strong and dependable; it will never take you off track or scramble your navigation system. God's path will never rob you of what you were supposed to have, or who you were intended to be. You can trust what He tells you in Isaiah 43:18-19, *"But forget all that"* (referring to the miracles of bringing Israel out of Egypt); *"it is nothing compared to what I am going to do. ^{19}For I am about to do something new. See, I have already begun! Do you not see it? I will make a pathway through the wilderness. I will create rivers in the dry wasteland"* (NLT).

When the children of Israel first left the slavery of Egypt they were ecstatic! They were breaking out of the ruts that Pharaoh had forced them into and realizing that he would no longer be able to rob them of the life that God intended. They were packing up all their stuff and jumping for joy about the adventures ahead in their new life of freedom. Then they got out into the desert a ways and realized that it was hot and dry, unfamiliar and overwhelming. There were bugs and snakes and they were always on the move! They couldn't relax! The water was scarce and they didn't like the food. So they became discontent and got mad at Moses for bringing them out of Egypt. Do you see what was happening there? Because life outside of captivity wasn't just what they expected, they focused on complaining instead of counting their blessings! They immediately forgot the dark and brutal designs of their Egyptian task masters and wanted to give up their freedom and go back to what they knew: hard bondage! It was fatal, but it was familiar. Their attitude was so poisoned and pathetic that it was obscuring the pathway! God was leading them to a Promised Land

Born to Privilege

of milk and honey, but because they had to get there by way of the wilderness they threw a fit! We don't get to choose the pathway that gets us to our Promised Land; but the events along the way are not lost on God. His provision for our journey will be more than sufficient, sisters; it will be perfect and complete. Nothing takes Him by surprise, and the timing of each segment is His to arrange.

Don't make the mistake of thinking you know best. Instead of trying to get God on board with your imperfect plan, step out of your ruts and old habits and become a part of His perfect ways. Let God do something brand new in you! Let the Shepherd lead you to green pastures and clear waters. It is time to work your way out of that 'old normal' cocoon and spread the wings of your New Normal as a daughter of the Most High, with all the exciting truths of this study in your backpack! Your new-found freedom may seem a bit scary at first, but once you get going you will never want to go back! Hoist that pack of provisions, lift your vision high, straighten that tiara, and fly free! You are on your way to the life of privilege that you were born for.

Theme Verse

Isaiah 43:19 (NLT): *"For I am about to do something new. See, I have already begun! Do you not see it? I will make a pathway through the wilderness. I will create rivers in the dry wasteland."*

Take-away Gems

- ♦ The Holy Spirit helps me to recognize His voice above all others.
- ♦ God's normal will balance my life and make me complete.
- ♦ Lord, your ways are perfect; do something new in me!

Own It!

Personalize: Think about your definition of 'normal'. How would you define a normal life? Do you think your life is normal?

If not, what circumstances, relationships and/or opportunities would change your mind?

Ponder: Write down your take-away gems for Chapter Eight in your journal or notebook. Choose your personal nugget for this chapter, either from your gems list or from elsewhere in the text, and write something about why you chose this concept. During your quiet time ask the Holy Spirit to help you embrace His New Normal and anticipate good things on the path ahead of you.

Pursue: Make a short list of any hesitations you feel inside about God's "normal". Next, be honest in admitting the reason and jotting it down beside each hesitation. Finally, use Scripture to recognize what provisions God has already given you for overcoming these; write these remedies down and thank God for them. Use a concordance, a topical Bible, or other study tools to find your scriptural remedies, remembering that God has answers for everything!

Persist: Take some quiet time to compare your past to Israel's bondage under the Egyptians. As you think of your freedom in Christ, picture yourself in the wilderness on the way to your Promised Land. What circumstances, real or imagined, would tempt you to complain about leaving the familiar territory of your past? Ask the Lord to help you trust Him on your path to the future.

Partner: In your Circle of Wagons, talk about the voices of the world. Choose some elements of life that are important to you such as family, career, God, spirituality, marriage, etc. and discuss how the world defines them. How do the world's definitions compare to the Bible? Exchange thoughts about what is most important in society versus what is most important to God. Discuss how human reasoning can be deceiving, and why spiritual discernment is necessary in prioritizing your life.

Now, go out there and be the best YOU that you can be!

About the Author

Rebecca Bryan-Howell has been writing poetry, songs, and stories from the young age of fourteen. Her stories and poetry are powerfully picturesque, as she uses the common elements of the family circle, church life, the essence of friendship, or a day in the neighborhood to create something artful and inspirational that will touch the soul with a delicate grace and the heart with brimming hope. Her writing aptly demonstrates the full spectrum of Life's encounters as she weaves laughter into tears and turns struggle into triumph, moving her readers to laugh, cry and identify with the human heartbeat of her script.

Gifted in exhortation and encouragement, Rebecca's real-life characterization of the classic, yet complex, human experience brings both wit and depth of soul into play, splashing sunshine into cloudy weather, fresh air into muggy circumstances, and hidden treasures along the worn and dusty Paths of Life to unlock eternal perspectives and make a lasting difference for her readers.

Her inspirational articles and Christian study materials spring from the strong Christian heritage that taught her to face mountains with determination, walk valleys with her eyes on Jesus, and navigate stormy seas with the compass of God's eternal Word. Supporting her readers on their own Path of Life, Becca delights to bring light, hope, and great expectation to all who will hear the Good News of the Christ who came to lift the fallen, mend broken hearts, heal the wounded, and comfort the weary.

She has published two poems, three books, and currently produces a semi-monthly photo blog while striving to maintain a writer's website where she posts excerpts of her diverse and ongoing literary works. You may go to *www.PrismOfLife.com* to subscribe for updates or visit her photo blog and sign up to follow her posts at *beccasbloominblog.wordpress.com*.

Rebecca will always write from her heart to yours – stories that are true, or should be. She says, "Any life provides writing material, but only the life where Jesus is Lord promises Happy Endings!" Becca invites you to come with her through the Garden of Life and follow her writing into places you have never been…or have never imagined you could go.

So, come along and enjoy the read!

Other books by the author

The Littlest Warrior
Where do babies go when they die? Follow Bradey through his Heavenly adventures in this charming story of hope, anticipation, and comfort for a mother's sorrowing heart…a sweet story wrapped in roses and rainbows!

A Song in the Night
In this true story that begins in the Old West, the pioneer roots planted in the Idaho Territory were strong and independent. Their seeds, scattered by the winds of time, grew in many directions; but one handful landed in the fertile soil of happy family adventures and grew into the story behind this book. Courage, adventure, homestead life, and lots of singing blaze this trail for hard decisions, frightening circumstances, stormy weather and life challenges that one little girl never even imagined going through. Eunice Christina's story weaves laughter with tears, joy with sorrow, and desperate hope with searing disappointment; because that's real life. Yet, when the deep pain of the weary soul is woven together with the rich music of a tender heart, miracles happen.

Made in the USA
Columbia, SC
03 July 2020